# TEACHER'S PET PUBLICATIONS

PUZZLE PACK
for
Much Ado About Nothing

based on the book by
William Shakespeare

Written by
Mary B. Collins

© 2007 Teacher's Pet Publications
All Rights Reserved

The materials in this packet are copyrighted
by Teacher's Pet Publications, Inc.

These pages may be duplicated by the purchaser
for use in the purchaser's own classroom.

Copying any of these materials and distributing them
for any other purpose is a violation of the copyright laws.

© 2007 Teacher's Pet Publications, Inc.
www.tpet.com

INTRODUCTION
If you already own the LitPlan for this title, this Puzzle Pack will refresh your Unit Resource Materials and Vocabulary Resource Materials sections plus give you additional materials you can substitute into the tests. If you do not already have a complete LitPlan, these pages will give you some supplemental materials to use with your own plan. There are two main groups of materials: one set for unit words (such as characters' names, symbols, places, etc.) and one set for vocabulary words associated with the book.

WORD LIST
There is a word list for both the unit words and the vocabulary words. These lists show you which words are being used in the materials and the clues or definitions being used for those words. You may want to give students a word list with clues/definitions to help them, or you may want students to only have a word list (without clues/definitions) if you want them to work a little harder. Both are available for duplication. The word lists can also be your "calling key" for the bingo games.

FILL IN THE BLANK AND MATCHING
There are 4 each of the fill in the blank and matching worksheets for both the unit and vocabulary words. These pages can be used either as extra worksheets for students or as objective parts of a unit test. They can be done individually if students need extra help or as a whole class activity to review the material covered.

MAGIC SQUARES
The magic squares not only reinforce the material covered but also work on reasoning and math skills. Many teachers have told us that their students really enjoy doing these!

WORD SEARCH PUZZLES
The word search words go in all directions, as indicated on your answer keys. Two of the word search puzzles have the clues listed rather than the words. This makes the puzzle a little more difficult, but it reinforces the material better. Two word search puzzles have words only for students who find the clue puzzles too difficult.

CROSSWORD PUZZLES
Both unit and vocabulary word sections have 4 crossword puzzles.

BINGO CARDS
There are 32 individual bingo cards for the unit words and 32 individual bingo cards for the vocabulary words. You can use your word list as a "call list," calling the words at random and marking them off of your list as you go, or you could use the flash cards by cutting them apart and drawing the words at random from a hat (or box or whatever). To make a better review, you might ask for the definition and spelling of each word as you call it out–or you could call out the definitions and have students tell you the words they need to look for on the puzzle.

JUGGLE LETTERS
The vocabulary juggle letter game is intended to help students learn the spellings of the words. One sheet has the definitions listed on it as an extra help for students who need it or to reinforce the definitions if you choose to do so.

FLASH CARDS
We've included a set of vocabulary flash cards you can duplicate, cut, and fold for your students. Some teachers make a few sets for general use by the class; others make a set for each student. Some teachers duplicate them for each student and have the students cut & fold their own. You can cut out just the words and put them in a hat, have each student pick out one word and write the definition and a sentence for that word. Students then swap words and papers, with the next student adding a sentence of his own under the last one. You can have students swap as many times as you like. Each time the student will read the sentences written prior to his own and then add a sentence. You can cut out the words and definitions separately and play "I Have; Who Has?" Each student in the room draws a word and definition. The first student says, "I have (the name of the word). Who has the definition?" The student with the definition reads it then says, "I have (the name of the vocabulary word she has). Who has the definition?" The round continues until all words and definitions have been given.

Much Ado About Nothing Word List

No.	Word	Clue/Definition
1.	ANTONIO	Governor's brother; uncle to Hero and Beatrice
2.	AVON	Shakespeare's home: Stratford-Upon-___
3.	BALTHASAR	He sings the songs in the play.
4.	BEATRICE	She and Benedick have a love-hate relationship.
5.	BENEDICK	He is tricked into thinking Beatrice loves him.
6.	BLANK	Unrhymed iambic pentameter: ___ verse
7.	BORACHIO	He visits Margaret in the night to deceive Claudio.
8.	CLAUDIO	He was to marry Hero.
9.	COMIC	This kind of relief breaks the emotional tension of a play.
10.	CONRAD	Borachio's sidekick
11.	DENOUNCES	Upon hearing the accusations, Leonato ___ Hero as his daughter.
12.	DIED	The Friar tells Leonato to publicly announce that Hero ____ after being accused.
13.	DOGBERRY	Constable of Messina
14.	DUCATS	Don John gave Borachio 1,000 of these for his part in the scheme.
15.	DUEL	Leonato challenges Claudio to one.
16.	FAINTS	What Hero does after denying Claudio's accusations
17.	FRIAR	He devises the plan to restore Hero's reputation.
18.	HERO	She is disgraced at the altar.
19.	HUSBAND	Beatrice says she is thankful to God every night that she doesn't have one.
20.	INSULTS	Beatrice hurls these at Benedick upon his arrival.
21.	JOHN	Don Pedro's villainous brother
22.	KILL	Beatrice wants Benedick to do this to Claudio for what he did to Hero.
23.	LAMENT	Sad song of regret, usually for a lost love
24.	LEONATO	Governor of Messina
25.	LOVE	Now that the war is over, Claudio is ready to think about this.
26.	MARGARET	She is seen at the window with Borachio.
27.	MARRY	Benedick swears he will never do this, but he later changes his mind.
28.	MESSINA	Setting of Much Ado
29.	ORANGE	Claudio calls Hero a rotten ____.
30.	PARTY	Leonato hosts a masquerade ____ at which the confusion in the play begins.
31.	PEDRO	Woos Leonato's daughter for another: Don ___
32.	SONNET	14 lined poem following ababcdcdefergg pattern
33.	TOOTHACHE	Benedick blames his melancholy behavior on this.
34.	VERGES	Constable's assistant
35.	WIFE	Benedick thinks a good ____ would be rich, wise, virtuous, fair, mild, noble, etc.
36.	WOO	Court with the intent to marry

Much Ado About Nothing Fill in the Blanks 1

_____

1. He visits Margaret in the night to deceive Claudio.
2. Benedick blames his melancholy behavior on this.
3. Leonato challenges Claudio to one.
4. Don Pedro's villainous brother
5. Sad song of regret, usually for a lost love
6. Court with the intent to marry
7. Governor of Messina
8. 14 lined poem following ababcdcdefergg pattern
9. Don John gave Borachio 1,000 of these for his part in the scheme.
10. She is disgraced at the altar.
11. This kind of relief breaks the emotional tension of a play.
12. What Hero does after denying Claudio's accusations
13. Setting of Much Ado
14. Constable of Messina
15. Shakespeare's home: Stratford-Upon-___
16. He devises the plan to restore Hero's reputation.
17. Unrhymed iambic pentameter: ___ verse
18. Beatrice says she is thankful to God every night that she doesn't have one.
19. Beatrice wants Benedick to do this to Claudio for what he did to Hero.
20. He sings the songs in the play.

Much Ado About Nothing Fill in the Blanks 1 Answer Key

BORACHIO	1. He visits Margaret in the night to deceive Claudio.
TOOTHACHE	2. Benedick blames his melancholy behavior on this.
DUEL	3. Leonato challenges Claudio to one.
JOHN	4. Don Pedro's villainous brother
LAMENT	5. Sad song of regret, usually for a lost love
WOO	6. Court with the intent to marry
LEONATO	7. Governor of Messina
SONNET	8. 14 lined poem following ababcdcdefergg pattern
DUCATS	9. Don John gave Borachio 1,000 of these for his part in the scheme.
HERO	10. She is disgraced at the altar.
COMIC	11. This kind of relief breaks the emotional tension of a play.
FAINTS	12. What Hero does after denying Claudio's accusations
MESSINA	13. Setting of Much Ado
DOGBERRY	14. Constable of Messina
AVON	15. Shakespeare's home: Stratford-Upon-___
FRIAR	16. He devises the plan to restore Hero's reputation.
BLANK	17. Unrhymed iambic pentameter: ___ verse
HUSBAND	18. Beatrice says she is thankful to God every night that she doesn't have one.
KILL	19. Beatrice wants Benedick to do this to Claudio for what he did to Hero.
BALTHASAR	20. He sings the songs in the play.

Much Ado About Nothing Fill in the Blanks 2

_____ 1. Governor of Messina

_____ 2. What Hero does after denying Claudio's accusations

_____ 3. Unrhymed iambic pentameter: ___ verse

_____ 4. He sings the songs in the play.

_____ 5. Governor's brother; uncle to Hero and Beatrice

_____ 6. Borachio's sidekick

_____ 7. Now that the war is over, Claudio is ready to think about this.

_____ 8. She is disgraced at the altar.

_____ 9. Setting of Much Ado

_____ 10. Court with the intent to marry

_____ 11. Constable of Messina

_____ 12. Benedick blames his melancholy behavior on this.

_____ 13. 14 lined poem following ababcdcdefergg pattern

_____ 14. Benedick swears he will never do this, but he later changes his mind.

_____ 15. Beatrice hurls these at Benedick upon his arrival.

_____ 16. Sad song of regret, usually for a lost love

_____ 17. He was to marry Hero.

_____ 18. The Friar tells Leonato to publicly announce that Hero ____ after being accused.

_____ 19. Leonato hosts a masquerade ____ at which the confusion in the play begins.

_____ 20. She and Benedick have a love-hate relationship.

Much Ado About Nothing Fill in the Blanks 2 Answer Key

LEONATO	1. Governor of Messina
FAINTS	2. What Hero does after denying Claudio's accusations
BLANK	3. Unrhymed iambic pentameter: ___ verse
BALTHASAR	4. He sings the songs in the play.
ANTONIO	5. Governor's brother; uncle to Hero and Beatrice
CONRAD	6. Borachio's sidekick
LOVE	7. Now that the war is over, Claudio is ready to think about this.
HERO	8. She is disgraced at the altar.
MESSINA	9. Setting of Much Ado
WOO	10. Court with the intent to marry
DOGBERRY	11. Constable of Messina
TOOTHACHE	12. Benedick blames his melancholy behavior on this.
SONNET	13. 14 lined poem following ababcdcdefergg pattern
MARRY	14. Benedick swears he will never do this, but he later changes his mind.
INSULTS	15. Beatrice hurls these at Benedick upon his arrival.
LAMENT	16. Sad song of regret, usually for a lost love
CLAUDIO	17. He was to marry Hero.
DIED	18. The Friar tells Leonato to publicly announce that Hero ____ after being accused.
PARTY	19. Leonato hosts a masquerade ____ at which the confusion in the play begins.
BEATRICE	20. She and Benedick have a love-hate relationship.

Much Ado About Nothing Fill in the Blanks 3

_____ 1. Beatrice wants Benedick to do this to Claudio for what he did to Hero.

_____ 2. Beatrice hurls these at Benedick upon his arrival.

_____ 3. Court with the intent to marry

_____ 4. Beatrice says she is thankful to God every night that she doesn't have one.

_____ 5. Borachio's sidekick

_____ 6. Sad song of regret, usually for a lost love

_____ 7. Shakespeare's home: Stratford-Upon-___

_____ 8. He was to marry Hero.

_____ 9. He devises the plan to restore Hero's reputation.

_____ 10. Governor's brother; uncle to Hero and Beatrice

_____ 11. He is tricked into thinking Beatrice loves him.

_____ 12. Benedick blames his melancholy behavior on this.

_____ 13. Claudio calls Hero a rotten ____.

_____ 14. She is disgraced at the altar.

_____ 15. Setting of Much Ado

_____ 16. He visits Margaret in the night to deceive Claudio.

_____ 17. Constable of Messina

_____ 18. She and Benedick have a love-hate relationship.

_____ 19. Leonato challenges Claudio to one.

_____ 20. Don John gave Borachio 1,000 of these for his part in the scheme.

Much Ado About Nothing Fill in the Blanks 3 Answer Key

KILL	1. Beatrice wants Benedick to do this to Claudio for what he did to Hero.
INSULTS	2. Beatrice hurls these at Benedick upon his arrival.
WOO	3. Court with the intent to marry
HUSBAND	4. Beatrice says she is thankful to God every night that she doesn't have one.
CONRAD	5. Borachio's sidekick
LAMENT	6. Sad song of regret, usually for a lost love
AVON	7. Shakespeare's home: Stratford-Upon-___
CLAUDIO	8. He was to marry Hero.
FRIAR	9. He devises the plan to restore Hero's reputation.
ANTONIO	10. Governor's brother; uncle to Hero and Beatrice
BENEDICK	11. He is tricked into thinking Beatrice loves him.
TOOTHACHE	12. Benedick blames his melancholy behavior on this.
ORANGE	13. Claudio calls Hero a rotten ____.
HERO	14. She is disgraced at the altar.
MESSINA	15. Setting of Much Ado
BORACHIO	16. He visits Margaret in the night to deceive Claudio.
DOGBERRY	17. Constable of Messina
BEATRICE	18. She and Benedick have a love-hate relationship.
DUEL	19. Leonato challenges Claudio to one.
DUCATS	20. Don John gave Borachio 1,000 of these for his part in the scheme.

Much Ado About Nothing Fill in the Blanks 4

_____ 1. Don John gave Borachio 1,000 of these for his part in the scheme.
_____ 2. What Hero does after denying Claudio's accusations
_____ 3. Court with the intent to marry
_____ 4. She is disgraced at the altar.
_____ 5. Borachio's sidekick
_____ 6. Unrhymed iambic pentameter: ___ verse
_____ 7. This kind of relief breaks the emotional tension of a play.
_____ 8. Beatrice says she is thankful to God every night that she doesn't have one.
_____ 9. Benedick blames his melancholy behavior on this.
_____ 10. Governor of Messina
_____ 11. He visits Margaret in the night to deceive Claudio.
_____ 12. She and Benedick have a love-hate relationship.
_____ 13. Leonato hosts a masquerade ____ at which the confusion in the play begins.
_____ 14. Benedick thinks a good ____ would be rich, wise, virtuous, fair, mild, noble, etc.
_____ 15. He is tricked into thinking Beatrice loves him.
_____ 16. 14 lined poem following ababcdcdefergg pattern
_____ 17. Woos Leonato's daughter for another: Don ___
_____ 18. Governor's brother; uncle to Hero and Beatrice
_____ 19. He was to marry Hero.
_____ 20. Don Pedro's villainous brother

Much Ado About Nothing Fill in the Blanks 4 Answer Key

DUCATS	1. Don John gave Borachio 1,000 of these for his part in the scheme.
FAINTS	2. What Hero does after denying Claudio's accusations
WOO	3. Court with the intent to marry
HERO	4. She is disgraced at the altar.
CONRAD	5. Borachio's sidekick
BLANK	6. Unrhymed iambic pentameter: ___ verse
COMIC	7. This kind of relief breaks the emotional tension of a play.
HUSBAND	8. Beatrice says she is thankful to God every night that she doesn't have one.
TOOTHACHE	9. Benedick blames his melancholy behavior on this.
LEONATO	10. Governor of Messina
BORACHIO	11. He visits Margaret in the night to deceive Claudio.
BEATRICE	12. She and Benedick have a love-hate relationship.
PARTY	13. Leonato hosts a masquerade ___ at which the confusion in the play begins.
WIFE	14. Benedick thinks a good ___ would be rich, wise, virtuous, fair, mild, noble, etc.
BENEDICK	15. He is tricked into thinking Beatrice loves him.
SONNET	16. 14 lined poem following ababcdcdefergg pattern
PEDRO	17. Woos Leonato's daughter for another: Don ___
ANTONIO	18. Governor's brother; uncle to Hero and Beatrice
CLAUDIO	19. He was to marry Hero.
JOHN	20. Don Pedro's villainous brother

Much Ado About Nothing Matching 1

___ 1. VERGES   A. She is disgraced at the altar.
___ 2. DUCATS   B. Constable's assistant
___ 3. COMIC   C. She and Benedick have a love-hate relationship.
___ 4. WIFE   D. What Hero does after denying Claudio's accusations
___ 5. ANTONIO   E. Beatrice says she is thankful to God every night that she doesn't have one.
___ 6. PEDRO   F. This kind of relief breaks the emotional tension of a play.
___ 7. FRIAR   G. Governor's brother; uncle to Hero and Beatrice
___ 8. HUSBAND   H. Woos Leonato's daughter for another: Don ___
___ 9. AVON   I. Unrhymed iambic pentameter: ___ verse
___10. MARRY   J. Benedick thinks a good ____ would be rich, wise, virtuous, fair, mild, noble, etc.
___11. MESSINA   K. Upon hearing the accusations, Leonato ___ Hero as his daughter.
___12. BENEDICK L. He visits Margaret in the night to deceive Claudio.
___13. LOVE   M. Benedick swears he will never do this, but he later changes his mind.
___14. BLANK   N. Shakespeare's home: Stratford-Upon-___
___15. BALTHASAR O. Don John gave Borachio 1,000 of these for his part in the scheme.
___16. MARGARET P. Sad song of regret, usually for a lost love
___17. BORACHIO Q. Governor of Messina
___18. DENOUNCES R. He is tricked into thinking Beatrice loves him.
___19. BEATRICE S. Constable of Messina
___20. DOGBERRY T. She is seen at the window with Borachio.
___21. FAINTS   U. Benedick blames his melancholy behavior on this.
___22. HERO   V. Setting of Much Ado
___23. LAMENT   W. He devises the plan to restore Hero's reputation.
___24. LEONATO   X. Now that the war is over, Claudio is ready to think about this.
___25. TOOTHACHE Y. He sings the songs in the play.

Much Ado About Nothing Matching 1 Answer Key

B - 1. VERGES		A. She is disgraced at the altar.
O - 2. DUCATS		B. Constable's assistant
F - 3. COMIC		C. She and Benedick have a love-hate relationship.
J - 4. WIFE		D. What Hero does after denying Claudio's accusations
G - 5. ANTONIO		E. Beatrice says she is thankful to God every night that she doesn't have one.
H - 6. PEDRO		F. This kind of relief breaks the emotional tension of a play.
W - 7. FRIAR		G. Governor's brother; uncle to Hero and Beatrice
E - 8. HUSBAND		H. Woos Leonato's daughter for another: Don ___
N - 9. AVON		I. Unrhymed iambic pentameter: ___ verse
M - 10. MARRY		J. Benedick thinks a good ___ would be rich, wise, virtuous, fair, mild, noble, etc.
V - 11. MESSINA		K. Upon hearing the accusations, Leonato ___ Hero as his daughter.
R - 12. BENEDICK		L. He visits Margaret in the night to deceive Claudio.
X - 13. LOVE		M. Benedick swears he will never do this, but he later changes his mind.
I - 14. BLANK		N. Shakespeare's home: Stratford-Upon-___
Y - 15. BALTHASAR		O. Don John gave Borachio 1,000 of these for his part in the scheme.
T - 16. MARGARET		P. Sad song of regret, usually for a lost love
L - 17. BORACHIO		Q. Governor of Messina
K - 18. DENOUNCES		R. He is tricked into thinking Beatrice loves him.
C - 19. BEATRICE		S. Constable of Messina
S - 20. DOGBERRY		T. She is seen at the window with Borachio.
D - 21. FAINTS		U. Benedick blames his melancholy behavior on this.
A - 22. HERO		V. Setting of Much Ado
P - 23. LAMENT		W. He devises the plan to restore Hero's reputation.
Q - 24. LEONATO		X. Now that the war is over, Claudio is ready to think about this.
U - 25. TOOTHACHE		Y. He sings the songs in the play.

Much Ado About Nothing Matching 2

___ 1. PARTY — A. Upon hearing the accusations, Leonato ___ Hero as his daughter.
___ 2. CONRAD — B. Leonato hosts a masquerade ____ at which the confusion in the play begins.
___ 3. DIED — C. Beatrice says she is thankful to God every night that she doesn't have one.
___ 4. VERGES — D. Don John gave Borachio 1,000 of these for his part in the scheme.
___ 5. MARGARET — E. Setting of Much Ado
___ 6. LAMENT — F. Beatrice hurls these at Benedick upon his arrival.
___ 7. BEATRICE — G. He visits Margaret in the night to deceive Claudio.
___ 8. DENOUNCES — H. Beatrice wants Benedick to do this to Claudio for what he did to Hero.
___ 9. BORACHIO — I. She and Benedick have a love-hate relationship.
___ 10. HERO — J. He sings the songs in the play.
___ 11. MESSINA — K. Benedick blames his melancholy behavior on this.
___ 12. DOGBERRY — L. Constable of Messina
___ 13. HUSBAND — M. What Hero does after denying Claudio's accusations
___ 14. WIFE — N. Benedick thinks a good ____ would be rich, wise, virtuous, fair, mild, noble, etc.
___ 15. PEDRO — O. Governor of Messina
___ 16. BALTHASAR — P. Court with the intent to marry
___ 17. BENEDICK — Q. He is tricked into thinking Beatrice loves him.
___ 18. KILL — R. Constable's assistant
___ 19. INSULTS — S. The Friar tells Leonato to publicly announce that Hero ____ after being accused.
___ 20. SONNET — T. She is disgraced at the altar.
___ 21. WOO — U. Borachio's sidekick
___ 22. TOOTHACHE — V. She is seen at the window with Borachio.
___ 23. LEONATO — W. Sad song of regret, usually for a lost love
___ 24. DUCATS — X. 14 lined poem following ababcdcdefergg pattern
___ 25. FAINTS — Y. Woos Leonato's daughter for another: Don ___

Much Ado About Nothing Matching 2 Answer Key

B - 1. PARTY	A. Upon hearing the accusations, Leonato ___ Hero as his daughter.
U - 2. CONRAD	B. Leonato hosts a masquerade ____ at which the confusion in the play begins.
S - 3. DIED	C. Beatrice says she is thankful to God every night that she doesn't have one.
R - 4. VERGES	D. Don John gave Borachio 1,000 of these for his part in the scheme.
V - 5. MARGARET	E. Setting of Much Ado
W - 6. LAMENT	F. Beatrice hurls these at Benedick upon his arrival.
I - 7. BEATRICE	G. He visits Margaret in the night to deceive Claudio.
A - 8. DENOUNCES	H. Beatrice wants Benedick to do this to Claudio for what he did to Hero.
G - 9. BORACHIO	I. She and Benedick have a love-hate relationship.
T - 10. HERO	J. He sings the songs in the play.
E - 11. MESSINA	K. Benedick blames his melancholy behavior on this.
L - 12. DOGBERRY	L. Constable of Messina
C - 13. HUSBAND	M. What Hero does after denying Claudio's accusations
N - 14. WIFE	N. Benedick thinks a good ____ would be rich, wise, virtuous, fair, mild, noble, etc.
Y - 15. PEDRO	O. Governor of Messina
J - 16. BALTHASAR	P. Court with the intent to marry
Q - 17. BENEDICK	Q. He is tricked into thinking Beatrice loves him.
H - 18. KILL	R. Constable's assistant
F - 19. INSULTS	S. The Friar tells Leonato to publicly announce that Hero ____ after being accused.
X - 20. SONNET	T. She is disgraced at the altar.
P - 21. WOO	U. Borachio's sidekick
K - 22. TOOTHACHE	V. She is seen at the window with Borachio.
O - 23. LEONATO	W. Sad song of regret, usually for a lost love
D - 24. DUCATS	X. 14 lined poem following ababcdcdefergg pattern
M - 25. FAINTS	Y. Woos Leonato's daughter for another: Don ___

Much Ado About Nothing Matching 3

___ 1. LEONATO A. Benedick thinks a good ____ would be rich, wise, virtuous, fair, mild, noble, etc.
___ 2. BORACHIO B. She and Benedick have a love-hate relationship.
___ 3. BEATRICE C. Claudio calls Hero a rotten ____.
___ 4. VERGES D. Governor's brother; uncle to Hero and Beatrice
___ 5. COMIC E. Don John gave Borachio 1,000 of these for his part in the scheme.
___ 6. HERO F. He visits Margaret in the night to deceive Claudio.
___ 7. MESSINA G. He is tricked into thinking Beatrice loves him.
___ 8. SONNET H. He was to marry Hero.
___ 9. PEDRO I. Benedick blames his melancholy behavior on this.
___ 10. DOGBERRY J. Constable's assistant
___ 11. DUCATS K. Shakespeare's home: Stratford-Upon-___
___ 12. AVON L. The Friar tells Leonato to publicly announce that Hero ____ after being accused.
___ 13. INSULTS M. Borachio's sidekick
___ 14. DIED N. Beatrice hurls these at Benedick upon his arrival.
___ 15. ORANGE O. 14 lined poem following ababcdcdefergg pattern
___ 16. ANTONIO P. This kind of relief breaks the emotional tension of a play.
___ 17. KILL Q. He devises the plan to restore Hero's reputation.
___ 18. BLANK R. Now that the war is over, Claudio is ready to think about this.
___ 19. WIFE S. Setting of Much Ado
___ 20. CONRAD T. She is disgraced at the altar.
___ 21. LOVE U. Woos Leonato's daughter for another: Don ___
___ 22. TOOTHACHE V. Unrhymed iambic pentameter: ___ verse
___ 23. BENEDICK W. Governor of Messina
___ 24. CLAUDIO X. Beatrice wants Benedick to do this to Claudio for what he did to Hero.
___ 25. FRIAR Y. Constable of Messina

Much Ado About Nothing Matching 3 Answer Key

W - 1. LEONATO	A.	Benedick thinks a good ____ would be rich, wise, virtuous, fair, mild, noble, etc.
F - 2. BORACHIO	B.	She and Benedick have a love-hate relationship.
B - 3. BEATRICE	C.	Claudio calls Hero a rotten ____.
J - 4. VERGES	D.	Governor's brother; uncle to Hero and Beatrice
P - 5. COMIC	E.	Don John gave Borachio 1,000 of these for his part in the scheme.
T - 6. HERO	F.	He visits Margaret in the night to deceive Claudio.
S - 7. MESSINA	G.	He is tricked into thinking Beatrice loves him.
O - 8. SONNET	H.	He was to marry Hero.
U - 9. PEDRO	I.	Benedick blames his melancholy behavior on this.
Y - 10. DOGBERRY	J.	Constable's assistant
E - 11. DUCATS	K.	Shakespeare's home: Stratford-Upon-____
K - 12. AVON	L.	The Friar tells Leonato to publicly announce that Hero ____ after being accused.
N - 13. INSULTS	M.	Borachio's sidekick
L - 14. DIED	N.	Beatrice hurls these at Benedick upon his arrival.
C - 15. ORANGE	O.	14 lined poem following ababcdcdefergg pattern
D - 16. ANTONIO	P.	This kind of relief breaks the emotional tension of a play.
X - 17. KILL	Q.	He devises the plan to restore Hero's reputation.
V - 18. BLANK	R.	Now that the war is over, Claudio is ready to think about this.
A - 19. WIFE	S.	Setting of Much Ado
M - 20. CONRAD	T.	She is disgraced at the altar.
R - 21. LOVE	U.	Woos Leonato's daughter for another: Don ____
I - 22. TOOTHACHE	V.	Unrhymed iambic pentameter: ____ verse
G - 23. BENEDICK	W.	Governor of Messina
H - 24. CLAUDIO	X.	Beatrice wants Benedick to do this to Claudio for what he did to Hero.
Q - 25. FRIAR	Y.	Constable of Messina

Much Ado About Nothing Matching 4

___ 1. SONNET
___ 2. LOVE
___ 3. DOGBERRY
___ 4. ANTONIO
___ 5. WOO
___ 6. BLANK
___ 7. LAMENT
___ 8. PEDRO
___ 9. DENOUNCES
___ 10. COMIC
___ 11. BEATRICE
___ 12. DUEL
___ 13. FAINTS
___ 14. DUCATS
___ 15. BENEDICK
___ 16. CLAUDIO
___ 17. BORACHIO
___ 18. LEONATO
___ 19. DIED
___ 20. PARTY
___ 21. VERGES
___ 22. JOHN
___ 23. WIFE
___ 24. CONRAD
___ 25. MESSINA

A. He was to marry Hero.
B. 14 lined poem following ababcdcdefergg pattern
C. Court with the intent to marry
D. Don Pedro's villainous brother
E. Upon hearing the accusations, Leonato ___ Hero as his daughter.
F. Unrhymed iambic pentameter: ___ verse
G. Leonato hosts a masquerade ____ at which the confusion in the play begins.
H. Leonato challenges Claudio to one.
I. Benedick thinks a good ____ would be rich, wise, virtuous, fair, mild, noble, etc.
J. Governor's brother; uncle to Hero and Beatrice
K. He is tricked into thinking Beatrice loves him.
L. The Friar tells Leonato to publicly announce that Hero ____ after being accused.
M. Sad song of regret, usually for a lost love
N. Constable's assistant
O. Now that the war is over, Claudio is ready to think about this.
P. He visits Margaret in the night to deceive Claudio.
Q. She and Benedick have a love-hate relationship.
R. Don John gave Borachio 1,000 of these for his part in the scheme.
S. Woos Leonato's daughter for another: Don ___
T. What Hero does after denying Claudio's accusations
U. Setting of Much Ado
V. This kind of relief breaks the emotional tension of a play.
W. Governor of Messina
X. Borachio's sidekick
Y. Constable of Messina

Much Ado About Nothing Matching 4 Answer Key

B - 1. SONNET	A.	He was to marry Hero.
O - 2. LOVE	B.	14 lined poem following ababcdcdefergg pattern
Y - 3. DOGBERRY	C.	Court with the intent to marry
J - 4. ANTONIO	D.	Don Pedro's villainous brother
C - 5. WOO	E.	Upon hearing the accusations, Leonato ___ Hero as his daughter.
F - 6. BLANK	F.	Unrhymed iambic pentameter: ___ verse
M - 7. LAMENT	G.	Leonato hosts a masquerade ____ at which the confusion in the play begins.
S - 8. PEDRO	H.	Leonato challenges Claudio to one.
E - 9. DENOUNCES	I.	Benedick thinks a good ____ would be rich, wise, virtuous, fair, mild, noble, etc.
V -10. COMIC	J.	Governor's brother; uncle to Hero and Beatrice
Q -11. BEATRICE	K.	He is tricked into thinking Beatrice loves him.
H -12. DUEL	L.	The Friar tells Leonato to publicly announce that Hero ____ after being accused.
T -13. FAINTS	M.	Sad song of regret, usually for a lost love
R -14. DUCATS	N.	Constable's assistant
K -15. BENEDICK	O.	Now that the war is over, Claudio is ready to think about this.
A -16. CLAUDIO	P.	He visits Margaret in the night to deceive Claudio.
P -17. BORACHIO	Q.	She and Benedick have a love-hate relationship.
W -18. LEONATO	R.	Don John gave Borachio 1,000 of these for his part in the scheme.
L -19. DIED	S.	Woos Leonato's daughter for another: Don ___
G -20. PARTY	T.	What Hero does after denying Claudio's accusations
N -21. VERGES	U.	Setting of Much Ado
D -22. JOHN	V.	This kind of relief breaks the emotional tension of a play.
I - 23. WIFE	W.	Governor of Messina
X -24. CONRAD	X.	Borachio's sidekick
U -25. MESSINA	Y.	Constable of Messina

Much Ado About Nothing Magic Squares 1

Match the definition with the vocabulary word. Put your answers in the magic squares below. When your answers are correct, all columns and rows will add to the same number.

A. VERGES
B. HUSBAND
C. HERO
D. CONRAD
E. AVON
F. MARRY
G. ORANGE
H. JOHN
I. CLAUDIO
J. BENEDICK
K. DIED
L. FAINTS
M. INSULTS
N. PARTY
O. WOO
P. LOVE

1. Beatrice says she is thankful to God every night that she doesn't have one.
2. Claudio calls Hero a rotten ____.
3. The Friar tells Leonato to publicly announce that Hero ____ after being accused.
4. Leonato hosts a masquerade ____ at which the confusion in the play begins.
5. Beatrice hurls these at Benedick upon his arrival.
6. What Hero does after denying Claudio's accusations
7. Don Pedro's villainous brother
8. Constable's assistant
9. Now that the war is over, Claudio is ready to think about this.
10. He was to marry Hero.
11. Shakespeare's home: Stratford-Upon-___
12. Borachio's sidekick
13. She is disgraced at the altar.
14. Benedick swears he will never do this, but he later changes his mind.
15. He is tricked into thinking Beatrice loves him.
16. Court with the intent to marry

A=	B=	C=	D=
E=	F=	G=	H=
I=	J=	K=	L=
M=	N=	O=	P=

Much Ado About Nothing Magic Squares 1 Answer Key

Match the definition with the vocabulary word. Put your answers in the magic squares below. When your answers are correct, all columns and rows will add to the same number.

A. VERGES
B. HUSBAND
C. HERO
D. CONRAD
E. AVON
F. MARRY
G. ORANGE
H. JOHN
I. CLAUDIO
J. BENEDICK
K. DIED
L. FAINTS
M. INSULTS
N. PARTY
O. WOO
P. LOVE

1. Beatrice says she is thankful to God every night that she doesn't have one.
2. Claudio calls Hero a rotten ____.
3. The Friar tells Leonato to publicly announce that Hero ____ after being accused.
4. Leonato hosts a masquerade ____ at which the confusion in the play begins.
5. Beatrice hurls these at Benedick upon his arrival.
6. What Hero does after denying Claudio's accusations
7. Don Pedro's villainous brother
8. Constable's assistant
9. Now that the war is over, Claudio is ready to think about this.
10. He was to marry Hero.
11. Shakespeare's home: Stratford-Upon-___
12. Borachio's sidekick
13. She is disgraced at the altar.
14. Benedick swears he will never do this, but he later changes his mind.
15. He is tricked into thinking Beatrice loves him.
16. Court with the intent to marry

A=8	B=1	C=13	D=12
E=11	F=14	G=2	H=7
I=10	J=15	K=3	L=6
M=5	N=4	O=16	P=9

Much Ado About Nothing Magic Squares 2

Match the definition with the vocabulary word. Put your answers in the magic squares below. When your answers are correct, all columns and rows will add to the same number.

A. DOGBERRY   E. LAMENT   I. VERGES   M. DIED
B. MESSINA   F. JOHN   J. KILL   N. ANTONIO
C. FRIAR   G. DUEL   K. DENOUNCES   O. PARTY
D. HERO   H. BEATRICE L. COMIC   P. HUSBAND

1. Leonato hosts a masquerade ____ at which the confusion in the play begins.
2. She is disgraced at the altar.
3. Beatrice wants Benedick to do this to Claudio for what he did to Hero.
4. Sad song of regret, usually for a lost love
5. Constable's assistant
6. Don Pedro's villainous brother
7. Beatrice says she is thankful to God every night that she doesn't have one.
8. He devises the plan to restore Hero's reputation.
9. She and Benedick have a love-hate relationship.
10. Upon hearing the accusations, Leonato ___ Hero as his daughter.
11. Constable of Messina
12. Governor's brother; uncle to Hero and Beatrice
13. Setting of Much Ado
14. The Friar tells Leonato to publicly announce that Hero ____ after being accused.
15. Leonato challenges Claudio to one.
16. This kind of relief breaks the emotional tension of a play.

A=	B=	C=	D=
E=	F=	G=	H=
I=	J=	K=	L=
M=	N=	O=	P=

Much Ado About Nothing Magic Squares 2 Answer Key

Match the definition with the vocabulary word. Put your answers in the magic squares below. When your answers are correct, all columns and rows will add to the same number.

A. DOGBERRY	E. LAMENT	I. VERGES	M. DIED
B. MESSINA	F. JOHN	J. KILL	N. ANTONIO
C. FRIAR	G. DUEL	K. DENOUNCES	O. PARTY
D. HERO	H. BEATRICE	L. COMIC	P. HUSBAND

1. Leonato hosts a masquerade ____ at which the confusion in the play begins.
2. She is disgraced at the altar.
3. Beatrice wants Benedick to do this to Claudio for what he did to Hero.
4. Sad song of regret, usually for a lost love
5. Constable's assistant
6. Don Pedro's villainous brother
7. Beatrice says she is thankful to God every night that she doesn't have one.
8. He devises the plan to restore Hero's reputation.
9. She and Benedick have a love-hate relationship.
10. Upon hearing the accusations, Leonato ___ Hero as his daughter.
11. Constable of Messina
12. Governor's brother; uncle to Hero and Beatrice
13. Setting of Much Ado
14. The Friar tells Leonato to publicly announce that Hero ____ after being accused.
15. Leonato challenges Claudio to one.
16. This kind of relief breaks the emotional tension of a play.

A=11	B=13	C=8	D=2
E=4	F=6	G=15	H=9
I=5	J=3	K=10	L=16
M=14	N=12	O=1	P=7

Much Ado About Nothing Magic Squares 3

Match the definition with the vocabulary word. Put your answers in the magic squares below. When your answers are correct, all columns and rows will add to the same number.

A. PEDRO
B. BORACHIO
C. DUCATS
D. FRIAR
E. COMIC
F. JOHN
G. MARRY
H. DOGBERRY
I. BEATRICE
J. LAMENT
K. HUSBAND
L. WOO
M. CONRAD
N. MARGARET
O. DUEL
P. HERO

1. Constable of Messina
2. Woos Leonato's daughter for another: Don ___
3. He visits Margaret in the night to deceive Claudio.
4. Benedick swears he will never do this, but he later changes his mind.
5. Sad song of regret, usually for a lost love
6. Leonato challenges Claudio to one.
7. She is disgraced at the altar.
8. She and Benedick have a love-hate relationship.
9. Beatrice says she is thankful to God every night that she doesn't have one.
10. She is seen at the window with Borachio.
11. Borachio's sidekick
12. Court with the intent to marry
13. This kind of relief breaks the emotional tension of a play.
14. He devises the plan to restore Hero's reputation.
15. Don John gave Borachio 1,000 of these for his part in the scheme.
16. Don Pedro's villainous brother

A=	B=	C=	D=
E=	F=	G=	H=
I=	J=	K=	L=
M=	N=	O=	P=

Much Ado About Nothing Magic Squares 3 Answer Key

Match the definition with the vocabulary word. Put your answers in the magic squares below. When your answers are correct, all columns and rows will add to the same number.

A. PEDRO   E. COMIC   I. BEATRICE   M. CONRAD
B. BORACHIO   F. JOHN   J. LAMENT   N. MARGARET
C. DUCATS   G. MARRY   K. HUSBAND   O. DUEL
D. FRIAR   H. DOGBERRY   L. WOO   P. HERO

1. Constable of Messina
2. Woos Leonato's daughter for another: Don ___
3. He visits Margaret in the night to deceive Claudio.
4. Benedick swears he will never do this, but he later changes his mind.
5. Sad song of regret, usually for a lost love
6. Leonato challenges Claudio to one.
7. She is disgraced at the altar.
8. She and Benedick have a love-hate relationship.
9. Beatrice says she is thankful to God every night that she doesn't have one.
10. She is seen at the window with Borachio.
11. Borachio's sidekick
12. Court with the intent to marry
13. This kind of relief breaks the emotional tension of a play.
14. He devises the plan to restore Hero's reputation.
15. Don John gave Borachio 1,000 of these for his part in the scheme.
16. Don Pedro's villainous brother

A=2	B=3	C=15	D=14
E=13	F=16	G=4	H=1
I=8	J=5	K=9	L=12
M=11	N=10	O=6	P=7

Much Ado About Nothing Magic Squares 4

Match the definition with the vocabulary word. Put your answers in the magic squares below. When your answers are correct, all columns and rows will add to the same number.

A. PEDRO   E. HUSBAND   I. BEATRICE   M. LOVE
B. FRIAR   F. BLANK   J. HERO   N. MARGARET
C. FAINTS   G. MESSINA   K. INSULTS   O. DENOUNCES
D. JOHN   H. LEONATO   L. WOO   P. COMIC

1. Woos Leonato's daughter for another: Don ___
2. She is seen at the window with Borachio.
3. She is disgraced at the altar.
4. Beatrice says she is thankful to God every night that she doesn't have one.
5. Setting of Much Ado
6. Court with the intent to marry
7. This kind of relief breaks the emotional tension of a play.
8. What Hero does after denying Claudio's accusations
9. Upon hearing the accusations, Leonato ___ Hero as his daughter.
10. Don Pedro's villainous brother
11. Governor of Messina
12. Beatrice hurls these at Benedick upon his arrival.
13. She and Benedick have a love-hate relationship.
14. Unrhymed iambic pentameter: ___ verse
15. He devises the plan to restore Hero's reputation.
16. Now that the war is over, Claudio is ready to think about this.

A= 1	B= 15	C= 8	D= 10
E= 4	F= 14	G= 5	H= 11
I= 13	J= 3	K= 12	L= 6
M= 16	N= 2	O= 9	P= 7

Much Ado About Nothing Magic Squares 4 Answer Key

Match the definition with the vocabulary word. Put your answers in the magic squares below. When your answers are correct, all columns and rows will add to the same number.

A. PEDRO	E. HUSBAND	I. BEATRICE	M. LOVE
B. FRIAR	F. BLANK	J. HERO	N. MARGARET
C. FAINTS	G. MESSINA	K. INSULTS	O. DENOUNCES
D. JOHN	H. LEONATO	L. WOO	P. COMIC

1. Woos Leonato's daughter for another: Don ___
2. She is seen at the window with Borachio.
3. She is disgraced at the altar.
4. Beatrice says she is thankful to God every night that she doesn't have one.
5. Setting of Much Ado
6. Court with the intent to marry
7. This kind of relief breaks the emotional tension of a play.
8. What Hero does after denying Claudio's accusations
9. Upon hearing the accusations, Leonato ___ Hero as his daughter.
10. Don Pedro's villainous brother
11. Governor of Messina
12. Beatrice hurls these at Benedick upon his arrival.
13. She and Benedick have a love-hate relationship.
14. Unrhymed iambic pentameter: ___ verse
15. He devises the plan to restore Hero's reputation.
16. Now that the war is over, Claudio is ready to think about this.

A=1	B=15	C=8	D=10
E=4	F=14	G=5	H=11
I=13	J=3	K=12	L=6
M=16	N=2	O=9	P=7

Much Ado About Nothing Word Search 1

```
W M A R R Y Z M B F B S C G Z S T X F Q
D O T N Q P Y M E A L F L O G Y J P R P
O Q O A T S D V A V J D A D M H Q H I V
G T G N D G N N T O V F U E J I D K A B
B A L T H A S A R N Y D D N J H C P R M
E S F O U F B R I B T J I O W P W A H X
R T A N S W E J C O B B O U T R L R E G
R S I I B N N V E R I Y P N L B S T R D
Y O N O A F E T C A N D U C A T S Y O T
G N T J N T D M Z C S Z J E T X D N R D
M N S L D S I H Q H U R C S J X M G A N
C E X W E J C B T I L W Q V C O X B N N
C T S D D O K T O O T H A C H E H N G K
Q O G S G M N T J K S S B H L M Y N E X
Y K N F I Y S A Q N Z N H K J G R F J G
H D G R V N D K T L W C D B N G P Y L C
R C U P A D A C C O Y M P I K R T M V N
Z G N E F D T T R C S P S T E W F Q L N
X P L B L A N K V E R G E S Y D I S O F
L A M E N T X C P W G D Z H X T V F V F
K I L L P E D R O M A R G A R E T S E J
```

14 lined poem following ababcdcdefergg pattern (6)
Beatrice hurls these at Benedick upon his arrival. (7)
Beatrice says she is thankful to God every night that she doesn't have one. (7)
Beatrice wants Benedick to do this to Claudio for what he did to Hero. (4)
Benedick blames his melancholy behavior on this. (9)
Benedick swears he will never do this, but he later changes his mind. (5)
Benedick thinks a good ____ would be rich, wise, virtuous, fair, mild, noble, etc. (4)
Borachio's sidekick (6)
Claudio calls Hero a rotten ____. (6)
Constable of Messina (8)
Constable's assistant (6)
Court with the intent to marry (3)
Don John gave Borachio 1,000 of these for his part in the scheme. (6)
Don Pedro's villainous brother (4)
Governor of Messina (7)
Governor's brother; uncle to Hero and Beatrice (7)
He devises the plan to restore Hero's reputation. (5)
He is tricked into thinking Beatrice loves him. (8)
He sings the songs in the play. (9)
He visits Margaret in the night to deceive Claudio. (8)
He was to marry Hero. (7)
Leonato challenges Claudio to one. (4)
Leonato hosts a masquerade ____ at which the confusion in the play begins. (5)
Now that the war is over, Claudio is ready to think about this. (4)
Sad song of regret, usually for a lost love (6)
Setting of Much Ado (7)
Shakespeare's home: Stratford-Upon-____ (4)
She and Benedick have a love-hate relationship. (8)
She is disgraced at the altar. (4)
She is seen at the window with Borachio. (8)
The Friar tells Leonato to publicly announce that Hero ____ after being accused. (4)
This kind of relief breaks the emotional tension of a play. (5)
Unrhymed iambic pentameter: ____ verse (5)
Upon hearing the accusations, Leonato ____ Hero as his daughter. (9)
What Hero does after denying Claudio's accusations (6)
Woos Leonato's daughter for another: Don ____ (5)

Much Ado About Nothing Word Search 1 Answer Key

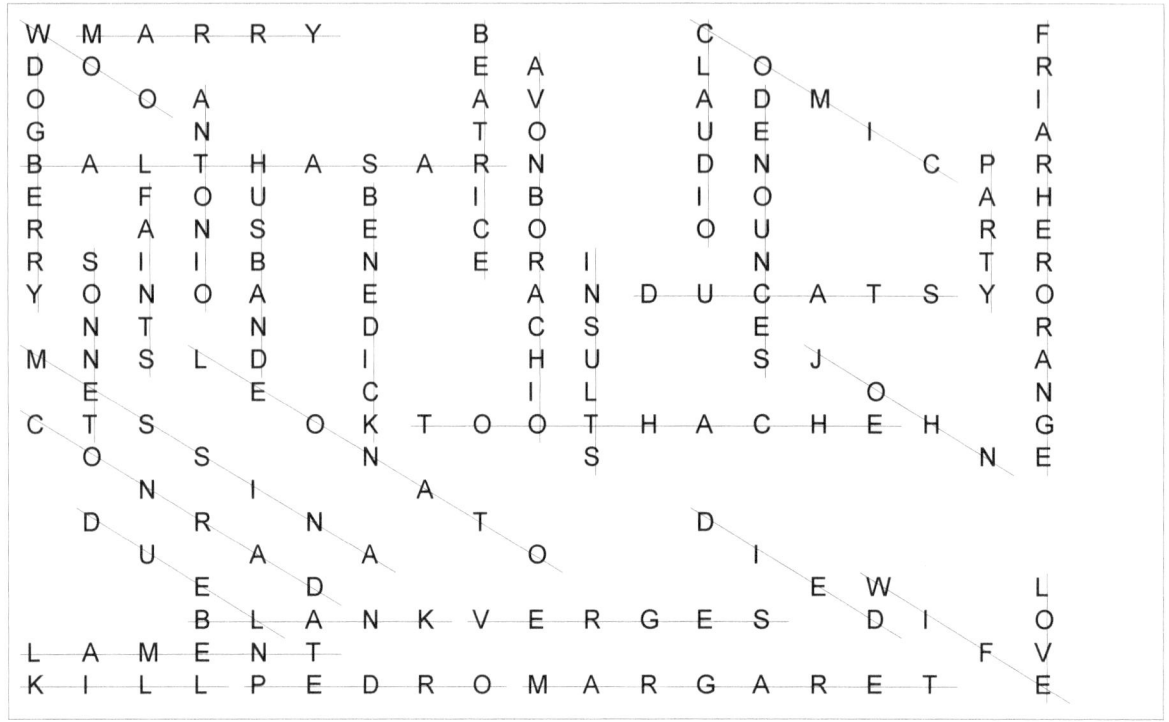

14 lined poem following ababcdcdefergg pattern (6)

Beatrice hurls these at Benedick upon his arrival. (7)

Beatrice says she is thankful to God every night that she doesn't have one. (7)

Beatrice wants Benedick to do this to Claudio for what he did to Hero. (4)

Benedick blames his melancholy behavior on this. (9)

Benedick swears he will never do this, but he later changes his mind. (5)

Benedick thinks a good ____ would be rich, wise, virtuous, fair, mild, noble, etc. (4)

Borachio's sidekick (6)

Claudio calls Hero a rotten ____. (6)

Constable of Messina (8)

Constable's assistant (6)

Court with the intent to marry (3)

Don John gave Borachio 1,000 of these for his part in the scheme. (6)

Don Pedro's villainous brother (4)

Governor of Messina (7)

Governor's brother; uncle to Hero and Beatrice (7)

He devises the plan to restore Hero's reputation. (5)

He is tricked into thinking Beatrice loves him. (8)

He sings the songs in the play. (9)

He visits Margaret in the night to deceive Claudio. (8)

He was to marry Hero. (7)

Leonato challenges Claudio to one. (4)

Leonato hosts a masquerade ____ at which the confusion in the play begins. (5)

Now that the war is over, Claudio is ready to think about this. (4)

Sad song of regret, usually for a lost love (6)

Setting of Much Ado (7)

Shakespeare's home: Stratford-Upon-___ (4)

She and Benedick have a love-hate relationship. (8)

She is disgraced at the altar. (4)

She is seen at the window with Borachio. (8)

The Friar tells Leonato to publicly announce that Hero ____ after being accused. (4)

This kind of relief breaks the emotional tension of a play. (5)

Unrhymed iambic pentameter: ___ verse (5)

Upon hearing the accusations, Leonato ___ Hero as his daughter. (9)

What Hero does after denying Claudio's accusations (6)

Woos Leonato's daughter for another: Don ___ (5)

Much Ado About Nothing Word Search 2

```
O B Z M K X L A M E N T L D F B I H F P
R L Y E R P O Y D H M P E E R A N E A H
A A L S Z T V K Y Y Z E O N I L S R I Y
N N S S C B E M I X N D N O A T U O N B
G K K I L O J B A L S R A U R H L B T L
E P D N F R M C X R L O T N Y A T E S K
T Y W A Q A T I F W R V O C M S S A K H
O W M P W C K V C S N Y W E C A X T L H
O L T G P H Q Y L N J Q P S M R D R L N
T Y V H N I Q L Z M R D P Q R Y S I C F
H G P N P O D O G B E R R Y T N C C K G
A H W Q H L M W S R T V R B G A O E W Q
C C B P M W T H W X X E S V G N N K L Z
H P E R G N P D T I S R G O J T R Z F K
E S N D B B Q C R L F G W D N O A S P X
D N E P V M A R G A R E T H L N D V B P
M Y D P R W L H X M K S P Z V I E M A Q
D R I J W B M W J Q N K W A Y O K T V P
U W C P O Y D H W V S W H F R Y W B O C
E B K P W H U S B A N D U C A T S O N J
L D I E D T N C L A U D I O B Y Y S O D
```

14 lined poem following ababcdcdefergg pattern (6)
Beatrice hurls these at Benedick upon his arrival. (7)
Beatrice says she is thankful to God every night that she doesn't have one. (7)
Beatrice wants Benedick to do this to Claudio for what he did to Hero. (4)
Benedick blames his melancholy behavior on this. (9)
Benedick swears he will never do this, but he later changes his mind. (5)
Benedick thinks a good ____ would be rich, wise, virtuous, fair, mild, noble, etc. (4)
Borachio's sidekick (6)
Claudio calls Hero a rotten ____. (6)
Constable of Messina (8)
Constable's assistant (6)
Court with the intent to marry (3)
Don John gave Borachio 1,000 of these for his part in the scheme. (6)
Don Pedro's villainous brother (4)
Governor of Messina (7)
Governor's brother; uncle to Hero and Beatrice (7)
He devises the plan to restore Hero's reputation. (5)
He is tricked into thinking Beatrice loves him. (8)

He sings the songs in the play. (9)
He visits Margaret in the night to deceive Claudio. (8)
He was to marry Hero. (7)
Leonato challenges Claudio to one. (4)
Leonato hosts a masquerade ____ at which the confusion in the play begins. (5)
Now that the war is over, Claudio is ready to think about this. (4)
Sad song of regret, usually for a lost love (6)
Setting of Much Ado (7)
Shakespeare's home: Stratford-Upon-___ (4)
She and Benedick have a love-hate relationship. (8)
She is disgraced at the altar. (4)
She is seen at the window with Borachio. (8)
The Friar tells Leonato to publicly announce that Hero ____ after being accused. (4)
This kind of relief breaks the emotional tension of a play. (5)
Unrhymed iambic pentameter: ___ verse (5)
Upon hearing the accusations, Leonato ___ Hero as his daughter. (9)
What Hero does after denying Claudio's accusations (6)
Woos Leonato's daughter for another: Don ___ (5)

Much Ado About Nothing Word Search 2 Answer Key

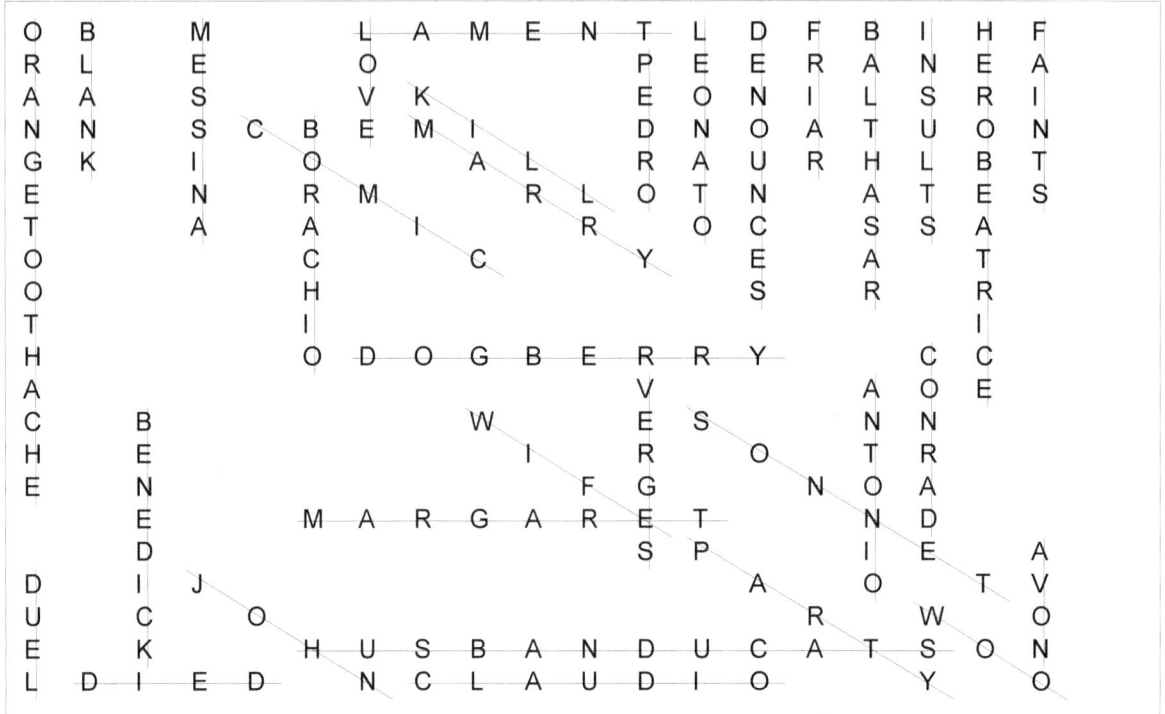

14 lined poem following ababcdcdefergg pattern (6)
Beatrice hurls these at Benedick upon his arrival. (7)
Beatrice says she is thankful to God every night that she doesn't have one. (7)
Beatrice wants Benedick to do this to Claudio for what he did to Hero. (4)
Benedick blames his melancholy behavior on this. (9)
Benedick swears he will never do this, but he later changes his mind. (5)
Benedick thinks a good ____ would be rich, wise, virtuous, fair, mild, noble, etc. (4)
Borachio's sidekick (6)
Claudio calls Hero a rotten ____. (6)
Constable of Messina (8)
Constable's assistant (6)
Court with the intent to marry (3)
Don John gave Borachio 1,000 of these for his part in the scheme. (6)
Don Pedro's villainous brother (4)
Governor of Messina (7)
Governor's brother; uncle to Hero and Beatrice (7)
He devises the plan to restore Hero's reputation. (5)
He is tricked into thinking Beatrice loves him. (8)

He sings the songs in the play. (9)
He visits Margaret in the night to deceive Claudio. (8)
He was to marry Hero. (7)
Leonato challenges Claudio to one. (4)
Leonato hosts a masquerade ____ at which the confusion in the play begins. (5)
Now that the war is over, Claudio is ready to think about this. (4)
Sad song of regret, usually for a lost love (6)
Setting of Much Ado (7)
Shakespeare's home: Stratford-Upon-____ (4)
She and Benedick have a love-hate relationship. (8)
She is disgraced at the altar. (4)
She is seen at the window with Borachio. (8)
The Friar tells Leonato to publicly announce that Hero ____ after being accused. (4)
This kind of relief breaks the emotional tension of a play. (5)
Unrhymed iambic pentameter: ____ verse (5)
Upon hearing the accusations, Leonato ____ Hero as his daughter. (9)
What Hero does after denying Claudio's accusations (6)
Woos Leonato's daughter for another: Don ____ (5)

Much Ado About Nothing Word Search 3

```
A V O N L E O N A T O M G J G I H B X V
D H M D B J Q R Z C J A V S W N U E J P
E C W O Z E K Y R F L R P F K S S N B Z
N J M G B L A M E N T G Y L S U B E A S
O M D B O G C T K N H A K N W L A D L D
U R D E R X W L R B F R V W D T N I T Z
N M Q R A Y F F A I R E P E F S D C H B
C H F R C Y S Z P U C T E R R R Y K A K
E M E Y H R C K H R D E D K V G I Q S X
S E W R I D H G Y M S I R F F H E A A L
P S T O O T H A C H E C O N R A D S R P
T S R B M Q V Q K T F T R C R W I O B R
J I R N C W Y M G R T Q A P J O D N J F
A N T O N I O J O H N B N Z D O U N T K
K A F D B F X R T T H L G L C M C E D S
I M D T X E P T M W H A E P D A A T U K
L N L G G S D S F W M N S J A R T W E K
L O V E C O M I C B X K F F K R S Y L V
K G N J D N M Y E Y Z N X K T Y T W L J
B C B L N D D Y B D Q C X H M N S Y F J
Q L B W J J W Y Y M M H J V Y M Z F D N
```

ANTONIO	COMIC	FRIAR	LOVE	TOOTHACHE
AVON	CONRAD	HERO	MARGARET	VERGES
BALTHASAR	DENOUNCES	HUSBAND	MARRY	WIFE
BEATRICE	DIED	INSULTS	MESSINA	WOO
BENEDICK	DOGBERRY	JOHN	ORANGE	
BLANK	DUCATS	KILL	PARTY	
BORACHIO	DUEL	LAMENT	PEDRO	
CLAUDIO	FAINTS	LEONATO	SONNET	

Much Ado About Nothing Word Search 3 Answer Key

ANTONIO	COMIC	FRIAR	LOVE	TOOTHACHE
AVON	CONRAD	HERO	MARGARET	VERGES
BALTHASAR	DENOUNCES	HUSBAND	MARRY	WIFE
BEATRICE	DIED	INSULTS	MESSINA	WOO
BENEDICK	DOGBERRY	JOHN	ORANGE	
BLANK	DUCATS	KILL	PARTY	
BORACHIO	DUEL	LAMENT	PEDRO	
CLAUDIO	FAINTS	LEONATO	SONNET	

Much Ado About Nothing Word Search 4

```
W K M P Q Z N K W A K W S K W O P K R R
J I B A A M D Z I N Z F N O L R K H W B
B L L A R K Y F T M B B C N A C Z Z D
D L O V E G T L E O N A T O F N M W O O
O R A O J T A Y T N D L R N D G E E R R
G D Q N R Y H R V I E T B R J E S T N Q
B I P T K N E I E O N H E A Y B S F H T
E E Q O W X R N R T O A N D P O I R U G
R D A O J B O S G X U S E Y H R N I S H
R C X T F X D U E J N A D C H A A B S
Y O L H R W H L S D C R I G N C B R A Y
T M K A K I N T W Z E L C V L H R J N C
C I G C U Z C S W Q S J K M C I W J D P
H C S H S D J E F A I N T S H O P X L F
N K C E P P I Q J J K Y B P M P E C C B
W C X X Z Y Y O H M X M Q F V F D R H B
D P H L J V Y M Q Y B W R H F M R T G R
F U J O H N D U C A T S P D N K O Q Q F
J F E L G C Z W G M N T V F K W W N G N
Z W Q L F V T C R W J H B S R B F J N K
R H S V T D B S X S K B C N J X C B R Z
```

ANTONIO	COMIC	FRIAR	LOVE	TOOTHACHE
AVON	CONRAD	HERO	MARGARET	VERGES
BALTHASAR	DENOUNCES	HUSBAND	MARRY	WIFE
BEATRICE	DIED	INSULTS	MESSINA	WOO
BENEDICK	DOGBERRY	JOHN	ORANGE	
BLANK	DUCATS	KILL	PARTY	
BORACHIO	DUEL	LAMENT	PEDRO	
CLAUDIO	FAINTS	LEONATO	SONNET	

Much Ado About Nothing Word Search 4 Answer Key

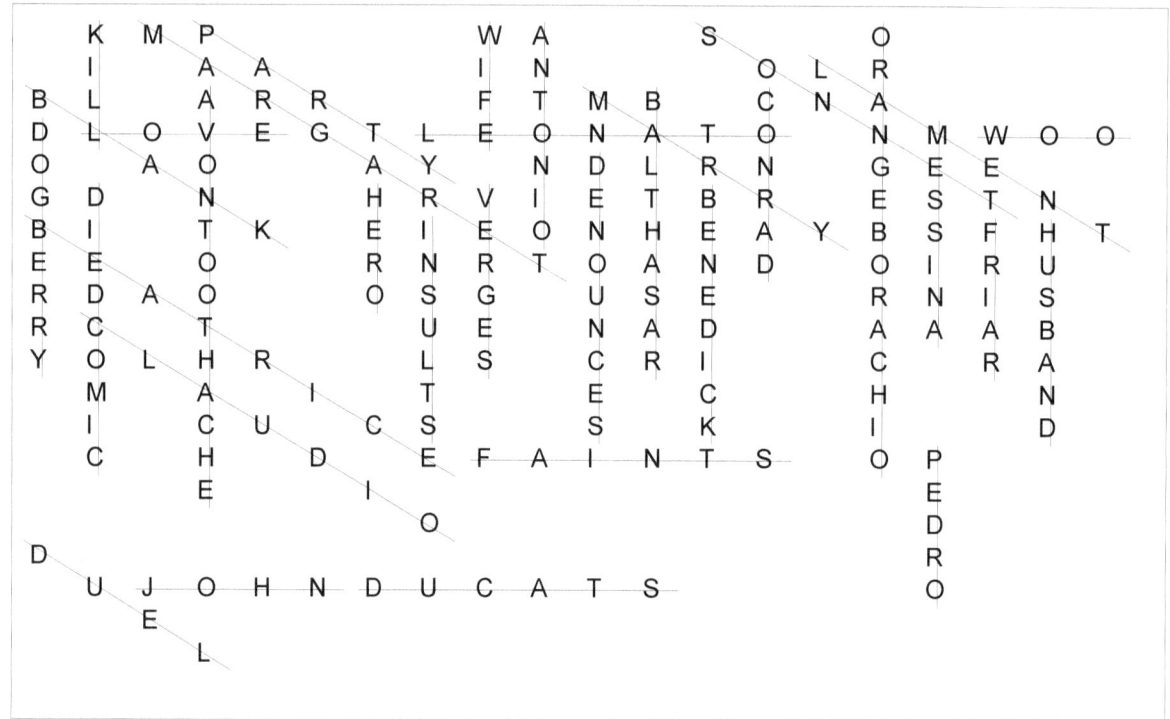

ANTONIO	COMIC	FRIAR	LOVE	TOOTHACHE
AVON	CONRAD	HERO	MARGARET	VERGES
BALTHASAR	DENOUNCES	HUSBAND	MARRY	WIFE
BEATRICE	DIED	INSULTS	MESSINA	WOO
BENEDICK	DOGBERRY	JOHN	ORANGE	
BLANK	DUCATS	KILL	PARTY	
BORACHIO	DUEL	LAMENT	PEDRO	
CLAUDIO	FAINTS	LEONATO	SONNET	

Much Ado About Nothing Crossword 1

Across
1. Governor's brother; uncle to Hero and Beatrice
4. This kind of relief breaks the emotional tension of a play.
6. Now that the war is over, Claudio is ready to think about this.
8. 14 lined poem following ababcdcdefergg pattern
9. He devises the plan to restore Hero's reputation.
10. Benedick thinks a good ____ would be rich, wise, virtuous, fair, mild, noble, etc.
15. She and Benedick have a love-hate relationship.
16. Don John gave Borachio 1,000 of these for his part in the scheme.
17. Leonato challenges Claudio to one.
18. Court with the intent to marry
19. Constable of Messina

Down
1. Shakespeare's home: Stratford-Upon-___
2. Benedick blames his melancholy behavior on this.
3. Beatrice hurls these at Benedick upon his arrival.
4. Borachio's sidekick
5. He was to marry Hero.
7. Constable's assistant
9. What Hero does after denying Claudio's accusations
11. Beatrice wants Benedick to do this to Claudio for what he did to Hero.
12. Woos Leonato's daughter for another: Don ___
13. Claudio calls Hero a rotten ____.
14. Beatrice says she is thankful to God every night that she doesn't have one.
15. Unrhymed iambic pentameter: ___ verse
17. The Friar tells Leonato to publicly announce that Hero ____ after being accused.

Much Ado About Nothing Crossword 1 Answer Key

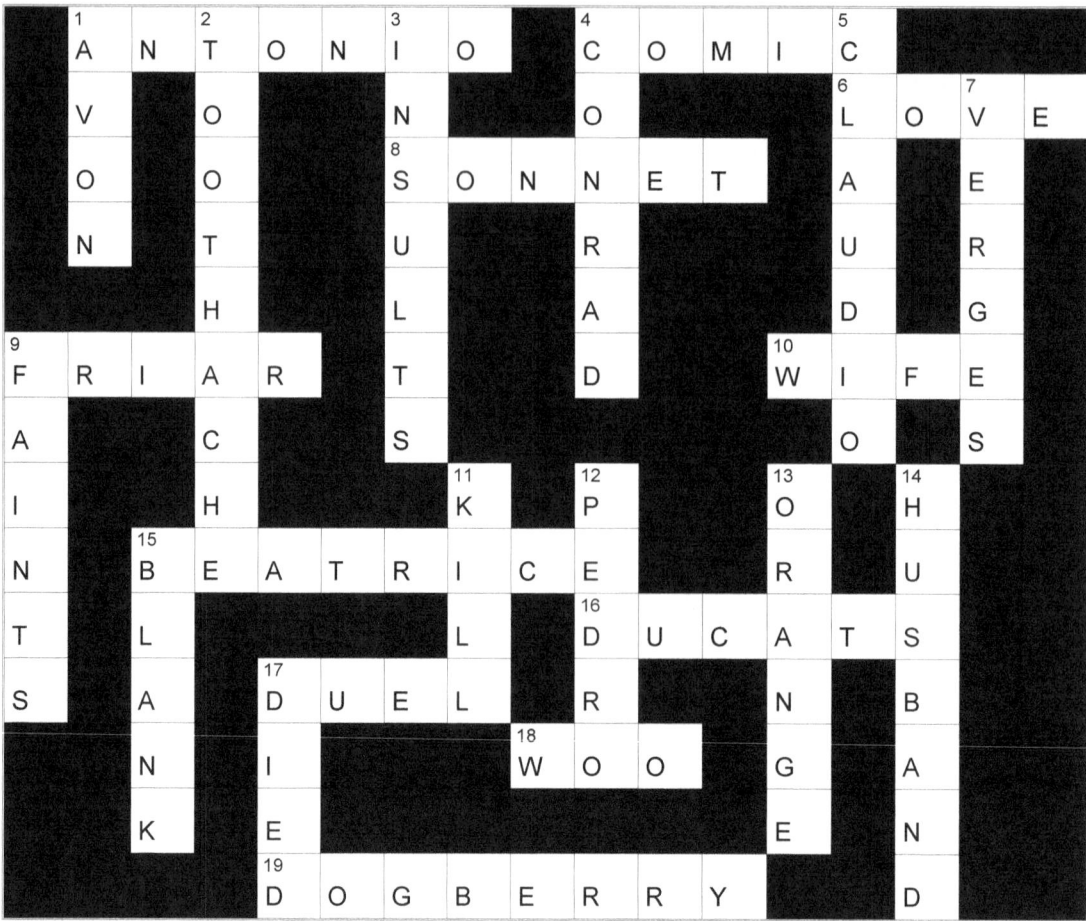

Across
1. Governor's brother; uncle to Hero and Beatrice
4. This kind of relief breaks the emotional tension of a play.
6. Now that the war is over, Claudio is ready to think about this.
8. 14 lined poem following ababcdcdefergg pattern
9. He devises the plan to restore Hero's reputation.
10. Benedick thinks a good ____ would be rich, wise, virtuous, fair, mild, noble, etc.
15. She and Benedick have a love-hate relationship.
16. Don John gave Borachio 1,000 of these for his part in the scheme.
17. Leonato challenges Claudio to one.
18. Court with the intent to marry
19. Constable of Messina

Down
1. Shakespeare's home: Stratford-Upon-___
2. Benedick blames his melancholy behavior on this.
3. Beatrice hurls these at Benedick upon his arrival.
4. Borachio's sidekick
5. He was to marry Hero.
7. Constable's assistant
9. What Hero does after denying Claudio's accusations
11. Beatrice wants Benedick to do this to Claudio for what he did to Hero.
12. Woos Leonato's daughter for another: Don ___
13. Claudio calls Hero a rotten ____.
14. Beatrice says she is thankful to God every night that she doesn't have one.
15. Unrhymed iambic pentameter: ___ verse
17. The Friar tells Leonato to publicly announce that Hero ____ after being accused.

Much Ado About Nothing Crossword 2

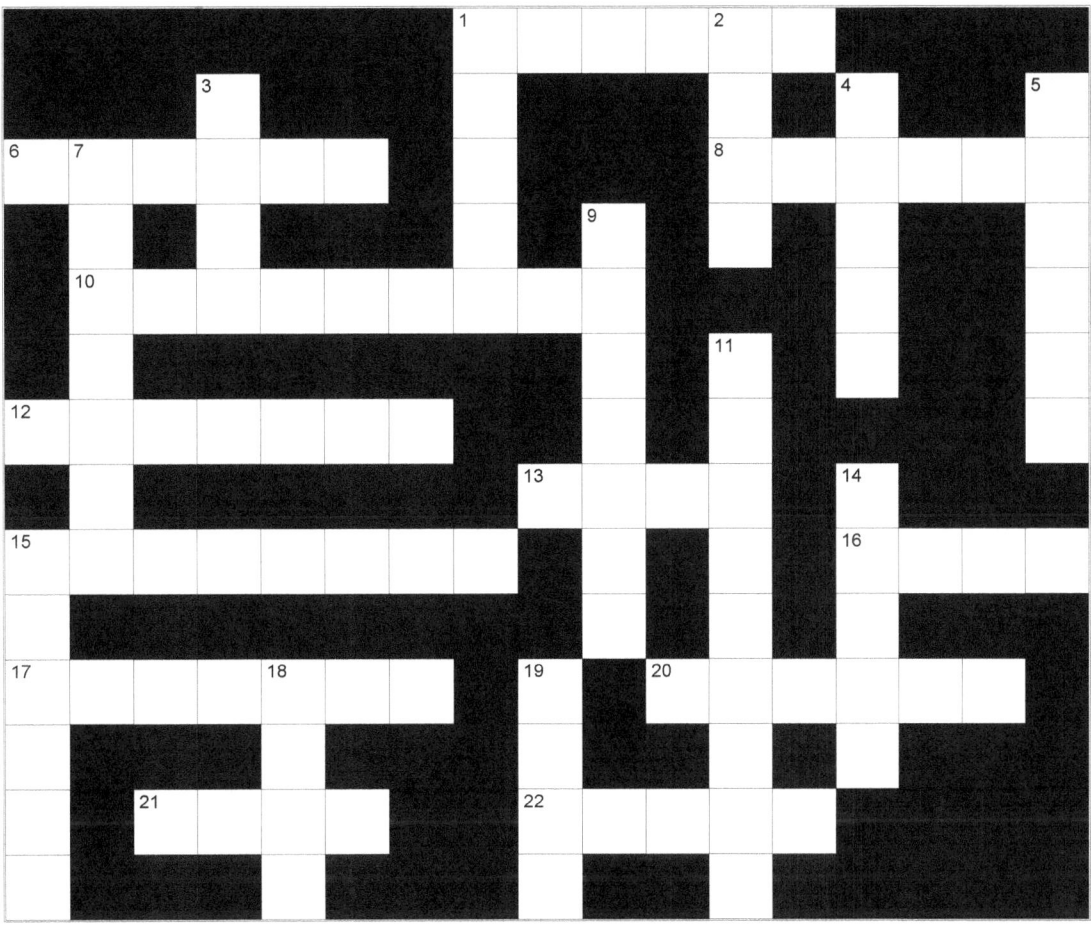

Across
1. Borachio's sidekick
6. Sad song of regret, usually for a lost love
8. Claudio calls Hero a rotten ____.
10. Benedick blames his melancholy behavior on this.
12. Beatrice hurls these at Benedick upon his arrival.
13. Beatrice wants Benedick to do this to Claudio for what he did to Hero.
15. Constable of Messina
16. Now that the war is over, Claudio is ready to think about this.
17. He was to marry Hero.
20. What Hero does after denying Claudio's accusations
21. The Friar tells Leonato to publicly announce that Hero ____ after being accused.
22. He devises the plan to restore Hero's reputation.

Down
1. This kind of relief breaks the emotional tension of a play.
2. Shakespeare's home: Stratford-Upon-___
3. She is disgraced at the altar.
4. Leonato hosts a masquerade ____ at which the confusion in the play begins.
5. Constable's assistant
7. Governor's brother; uncle to Hero and Beatrice
9. Setting of Much Ado
11. He sings the songs in the play.
14. Unrhymed iambic pentameter: ___ verse
15. Don John gave Borachio 1,000 of these for his part in the scheme.
18. Leonato challenges Claudio to one.
19. Benedick thinks a good ____ would be rich, wise, virtuous, fair, mild, noble, etc.

Much Ado About Nothing Crossword 2 Answer Key

Across
1. Borachio's sidekick
6. Sad song of regret, usually for a lost love
8. Claudio calls Hero a rotten ____.
10. Benedick blames his melancholy behavior on this.
12. Beatrice hurls these at Benedick upon his arrival.
13. Beatrice wants Benedick to do this to Claudio for what he did to Hero.
15. Constable of Messina
16. Now that the war is over, Claudio is ready to think about this.
17. He was to marry Hero.
20. What Hero does after denying Claudio's accusations
21. The Friar tells Leonato to publicly announce that Hero ____ after being accused.
22. He devises the plan to restore Hero's reputation.

Down
1. This kind of relief breaks the emotional tension of a play.
2. Shakespeare's home: Stratford-Upon-___
3. She is disgraced at the altar.
4. Leonato hosts a masquerade ____ at which the confusion in the play begins.
5. Constable's assistant
7. Governor's brother; uncle to Hero and Beatrice
9. Setting of Much Ado
11. He sings the songs in the play.
14. Unrhymed iambic pentameter: ___ verse
15. Don John gave Borachio 1,000 of these for his part in the scheme.
18. Leonato challenges Claudio to one.
19. Benedick thinks a good ____ would be rich, wise, virtuous, fair, mild, noble, etc.

Much Ado About Nothing Crossword 3

Across

1. Constable of Messina
2. This kind of relief breaks the emotional tension of a play.
4. Now that the war is over, Claudio is ready to think about this.
5. Sad song of regret, usually for a lost love
9. Don John gave Borachio 1,000 of these for his part in the scheme.
11. 14 lined poem following ababcdcdefergg pattern
12. Governor's brother; uncle to Hero and Beatrice
15. Beatrice says she is thankful to God every night that she doesn't have one.
17. She is seen at the window with Borachio.
18. Woos Leonato's daughter for another: Don ___
19. Beatrice wants Benedick to do this to Claudio for what he did to Hero.

Down

1. Leonato challenges Claudio to one.
2. Borachio's sidekick
3. He was to marry Hero.
6. Setting of Much Ado
7. What Hero does after denying Claudio's accusations
8. The Friar tells Leonato to publicly announce that Hero ____ after being accused.
10. Shakespeare's home: Stratford-Upon-___
13. Leonato hosts a masquerade ____ at which the confusion in the play begins.
14. Constable's assistant
15. She is disgraced at the altar.
16. Unrhymed iambic pentameter: ___ verse
17. Benedick swears he will never do this, but he later changes his mind.

Much Ado About Nothing Crossword 3 Answer Key

Across
1. Constable of Messina
2. This kind of relief breaks the emotional tension of a play.
4. Now that the war is over, Claudio is ready to think about this.
5. Sad song of regret, usually for a lost love
9. Don John gave Borachio 1,000 of these for his part in the scheme.
11. 14 lined poem following ababcdcdefergg pattern
12. Governor's brother; uncle to Hero and Beatrice
15. Beatrice says she is thankful to God every night that she doesn't have one.
17. She is seen at the window with Borachio.
18. Woos Leonato's daughter for another: Don ___
19. Beatrice wants Benedick to do this to Claudio for what he did to Hero.

Down
1. Leonato challenges Claudio to one.
2. Borachio's sidekick
3. He was to marry Hero.
6. Setting of Much Ado
7. What Hero does after denying Claudio's accusations
8. The Friar tells Leonato to publicly announce that Hero ____ after being accused.
10. Shakespeare's home: Stratford-Upon-___
13. Leonato hosts a masquerade ____ at which the confusion in the play begins.
14. Constable's assistant
15. She is disgraced at the altar.
16. Unrhymed iambic pentameter: ___ verse
17. Benedick swears he will never do this, but he later changes his mind.

Much Ado About Nothing Crossword 4

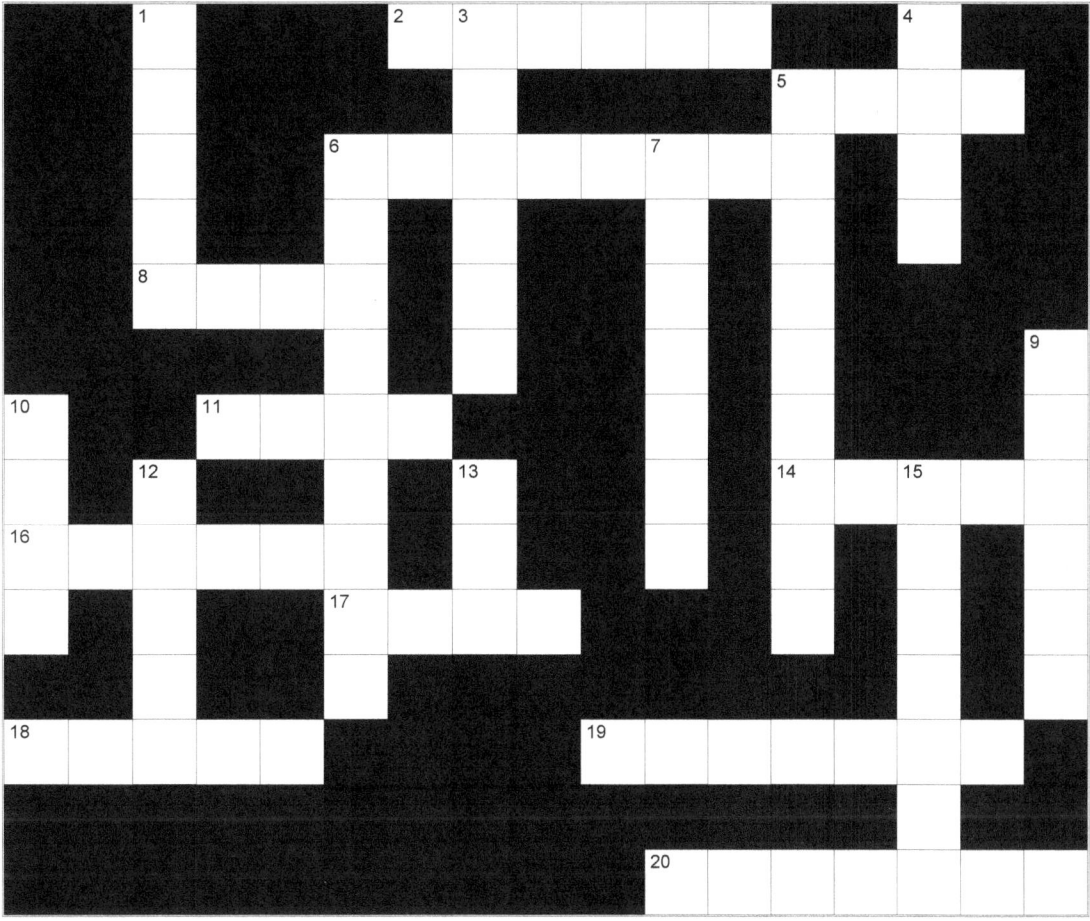

Across
2. 14 lined poem following ababcdcdefergg pattern
5. The Friar tells Leonato to publicly announce that Hero ____ after being accused.
6. She and Benedick have a love-hate relationship.
8. Beatrice wants Benedick to do this to Claudio for what he did to Hero.
11. Don Pedro's villainous brother
14. This kind of relief breaks the emotional tension of a play.
16. Constable's assistant
17. Shakespeare's home: Stratford-Upon-____
18. Leonato hosts a masquerade ____ at which the confusion in the play begins.
19. Governor's brother; uncle to Hero and Beatrice
20. Beatrice says she is thankful to God every night that she doesn't have one.

Down
1. Unrhymed iambic pentameter: ____ verse
3. Claudio calls Hero a rotten ____.
4. She is disgraced at the altar.
5. Upon hearing the accusations, Leonato ____ Hero as his daughter.
6. He sings the songs in the play.
7. Beatrice hurls these at Benedick upon his arrival.
9. Don John gave Borachio 1,000 of these for his part in the scheme.
10. Now that the war is over, Claudio is ready to think about this.
12. He devises the plan to restore Hero's reputation.
13. Court with the intent to marry
15. Setting of Much Ado

Much Ado About Nothing Crossword 4 Answer Key

Across
2. 14 lined poem following ababcdcdefergg pattern
5. The Friar tells Leonato to publicly announce that Hero ____ after being accused.
6. She and Benedick have a love-hate relationship.
8. Beatrice wants Benedick to do this to Claudio for what he did to Hero.
11. Don Pedro's villainous brother
14. This kind of relief breaks the emotional tension of a play.
16. Constable's assistant
17. Shakespeare's home: Stratford-Upon-____
18. Leonato hosts a masquerade ____ at which the confusion in the play begins.
19. Governor's brother; uncle to Hero and Beatrice
20. Beatrice says she is thankful to God every night that she doesn't have one.

Down
1. Unrhymed iambic pentameter: ____ verse
3. Claudio calls Hero a rotten ____.
4. She is disgraced at the altar.
5. Upon hearing the accusations, Leonato ___ Hero as his daughter.
6. He sings the songs in the play.
7. Beatrice hurls these at Benedick upon his arrival.
9. Don John gave Borachio 1,000 of these for his part in the scheme.
10. Now that the war is over, Claudio is ready to think about this.
12. He devises the plan to restore Hero's reputation.
13. Court with the intent to marry
15. Setting of Much Ado

Much Ado About Nothing

DUCATS	DENOUNCES	BLANK	DOGBERRY	SONNET
BENEDICK	ANTONIO	BALTHASAR	WIFE	VERGES
JOHN	PARTY	FREE SPACE	MESSINA	AVON
TOOTHACHE	HERO	FAINTS	HUSBAND	PEDRO
DIED	COMIC	LEONATO	MARGARET	MARRY

Much Ado About Nothing

BEATRICE	BORACHIO	CONRAD	ORANGE	KILL
LOVE	INSULTS	CLAUDIO	FRIAR	DUEL
WOO	MARRY	FREE SPACE	LEONATO	COMIC
DIED	PEDRO	HUSBAND	FAINTS	HERO
TOOTHACHE	AVON	MESSINA	LAMENT	PARTY

Much Ado About Nothing

HUSBAND	LEONATO	COMIC	FAINTS	AVON
HERO	DENOUNCES	DUEL	CONRAD	INSULTS
PEDRO	MESSINA	FREE SPACE	DIED	JOHN
TOOTHACHE	DOGBERRY	BEATRICE	FRIAR	MARRY
MARGARET	PARTY	DUCATS	KILL	SONNET

Much Ado About Nothing

ANTONIO	LAMENT	BENEDICK	WOO	BALTHASAR
BLANK	BORACHIO	ORANGE	WIFE	CLAUDIO
LOVE	SONNET	FREE SPACE	DUCATS	PARTY
MARGARET	MARRY	FRIAR	BEATRICE	DOGBERRY
TOOTHACHE	JOHN	DIED	VERGES	MESSINA

Much Ado About Nothing

DUEL	WOO	HUSBAND	LOVE	CLAUDIO
LAMENT	HERO	BEATRICE	FAINTS	DIED
ORANGE	MESSINA	FREE SPACE	DOGBERRY	JOHN
CONRAD	SONNET	PEDRO	KILL	BALTHASAR
BLANK	DENOUNCES	VERGES	COMIC	MARRY

Much Ado About Nothing

AVON	FRIAR	TOOTHACHE	BENEDICK	WIFE
DUCATS	LEONATO	ANTONIO	INSULTS	BORACHIO
MARGARET	MARRY	FREE SPACE	VERGES	DENOUNCES
BLANK	BALTHASAR	KILL	PEDRO	SONNET
CONRAD	JOHN	DOGBERRY	PARTY	MESSINA

Much Ado About Nothing

VERGES	AVON	PARTY	DUEL	COMIC
ANTONIO	DENOUNCES	BLANK	JOHN	LEONATO
ORANGE	PEDRO	FREE SPACE	BORACHIO	LOVE
WIFE	DOGBERRY	MESSINA	MARRY	CLAUDIO
SONNET	HUSBAND	TOOTHACHE	HERO	BALTHASAR

Much Ado About Nothing

BENEDICK	KILL	INSULTS	WOO	DIED
FAINTS	DUCATS	MARGARET	CONRAD	FRIAR
LAMENT	BALTHASAR	FREE SPACE	TOOTHACHE	HUSBAND
SONNET	CLAUDIO	MARRY	MESSINA	DOGBERRY
WIFE	LOVE	BORACHIO	BEATRICE	PEDRO

Much Ado About Nothing

FAINTS	FRIAR	CONRAD	JOHN	BLANK
BENEDICK	DENOUNCES	AVON	ORANGE	PARTY
BALTHASAR	DUCATS	FREE SPACE	LEONATO	DUEL
DIED	TOOTHACHE	SONNET	LOVE	HERO
WOO	LAMENT	ANTONIO	VERGES	BORACHIO

Much Ado About Nothing

MARRY	BEATRICE	MESSINA	INSULTS	HUSBAND
CLAUDIO	MARGARET	COMIC	PEDRO	WIFE
DOGBERRY	BORACHIO	FREE SPACE	ANTONIO	LAMENT
WOO	HERO	LOVE	SONNET	TOOTHACHE
DIED	DUEL	LEONATO	KILL	DUCATS

Much Ado About Nothing

LEONATO	HERO	HUSBAND	CONRAD	INSULTS
BLANK	PEDRO	JOHN	AVON	BENEDICK
BEATRICE	BALTHASAR	FREE SPACE	SONNET	KILL
DUEL	BORACHIO	DOGBERRY	DIED	LOVE
MESSINA	WOO	PARTY	FRIAR	TOOTHACHE

Much Ado About Nothing

MARRY	FAINTS	VERGES	COMIC	LAMENT
WIFE	ORANGE	MARGARET	ANTONIO	DUCATS
DENOUNCES	TOOTHACHE	FREE SPACE	PARTY	WOO
MESSINA	LOVE	DIED	DOGBERRY	BORACHIO
DUEL	KILL	SONNET	CLAUDIO	BALTHASAR

Much Ado About Nothing

MARRY	ORANGE	WIFE	LEONATO	INSULTS
SONNET	FAINTS	MARGARET	CLAUDIO	ANTONIO
BEATRICE	DOGBERRY	FREE SPACE	CONRAD	DIED
BALTHASAR	AVON	BENEDICK	PEDRO	VERGES
LAMENT	TOOTHACHE	DUCATS	DENOUNCES	DUEL

Much Ado About Nothing

HERO	BLANK	FRIAR	LOVE	MESSINA
HUSBAND	JOHN	KILL	WOO	BORACHIO
PARTY	DUEL	FREE SPACE	DUCATS	TOOTHACHE
LAMENT	VERGES	PEDRO	BENEDICK	AVON
BALTHASAR	DIED	CONRAD	COMIC	DOGBERRY

Much Ado About Nothing

WIFE	ANTONIO	JOHN	HERO	MESSINA
CONRAD	FAINTS	LAMENT	INSULTS	LEONATO
BEATRICE	HUSBAND	FREE SPACE	DIED	KILL
SONNET	PEDRO	MARRY	FRIAR	BLANK
LOVE	BENEDICK	WOO	DOGBERRY	VERGES

Much Ado About Nothing

DUEL	BORACHIO	AVON	ORANGE	MARGARET
BALTHASAR	CLAUDIO	COMIC	PARTY	DENOUNCES
DUCATS	VERGES	FREE SPACE	WOO	BENEDICK
LOVE	BLANK	FRIAR	MARRY	PEDRO
SONNET	KILL	DIED	TOOTHACHE	HUSBAND

Much Ado About Nothing

TOOTHACHE	CONRAD	DUCATS	DENOUNCES	LOVE
ANTONIO	PARTY	ORANGE	PEDRO	MESSINA
LAMENT	DUEL	FREE SPACE	WOO	DOGBERRY
WIFE	FAINTS	INSULTS	DIED	VERGES
SONNET	KILL	AVON	BORACHIO	HERO

Much Ado About Nothing

BALTHASAR	COMIC	LEONATO	MARRY	JOHN
CLAUDIO	BENEDICK	MARGARET	FRIAR	HUSBAND
BEATRICE	HERO	FREE SPACE	AVON	KILL
SONNET	VERGES	DIED	INSULTS	FAINTS
WIFE	DOGBERRY	WOO	BLANK	DUEL

Much Ado About Nothing

KILL	BALTHASAR	ORANGE	HERO	INSULTS
WIFE	PARTY	MARGARET	LEONATO	DOGBERRY
MARRY	FAINTS	FREE SPACE	BENEDICK	JOHN
MESSINA	BEATRICE	DENOUNCES	ANTONIO	HUSBAND
SONNET	LOVE	WOO	DIED	PEDRO

Much Ado About Nothing

FRIAR	DUEL	BLANK	BORACHIO	CLAUDIO
AVON	LAMENT	TOOTHACHE	DUCATS	CONRAD
VERGES	PEDRO	FREE SPACE	WOO	LOVE
SONNET	HUSBAND	ANTONIO	DENOUNCES	BEATRICE
MESSINA	JOHN	BENEDICK	COMIC	FAINTS

Much Ado About Nothing

DENOUNCES	BEATRICE	BENEDICK	SONNET	WOO
HERO	COMIC	INSULTS	DOGBERRY	BORACHIO
FRIAR	TOOTHACHE	FREE SPACE	VERGES	ANTONIO
ORANGE	KILL	JOHN	BLANK	DUEL
LEONATO	LOVE	CONRAD	MARGARET	HUSBAND

Much Ado About Nothing

LAMENT	DIED	WIFE	PEDRO	AVON
DUCATS	BALTHASAR	MARRY	CLAUDIO	FAINTS
MESSINA	HUSBAND	FREE SPACE	CONRAD	LOVE
LEONATO	DUEL	BLANK	JOHN	KILL
ORANGE	ANTONIO	VERGES	PARTY	TOOTHACHE

Much Ado About Nothing

AVON	BALTHASAR	WOO	TOOTHACHE	WIFE
INSULTS	MESSINA	COMIC	JOHN	BLANK
FAINTS	BEATRICE	FREE SPACE	BENEDICK	KILL
VERGES	PEDRO	LOVE	CLAUDIO	DUEL
MARGARET	MARRY	ANTONIO	DENOUNCES	HERO

Much Ado About Nothing

DOGBERRY	DUCATS	FRIAR	BORACHIO	PARTY
ORANGE	DIED	SONNET	CONRAD	LEONATO
HUSBAND	HERO	FREE SPACE	ANTONIO	MARRY
MARGARET	DUEL	CLAUDIO	LOVE	PEDRO
VERGES	KILL	BENEDICK	LAMENT	BEATRICE

Much Ado About Nothing

HERO	BENEDICK	PARTY	COMIC	LOVE
WIFE	KILL	MARGARET	CONRAD	TOOTHACHE
CLAUDIO	LEONATO	FREE SPACE	MESSINA	BORACHIO
ANTONIO	DUEL	VERGES	BALTHASAR	BEATRICE
DIED	JOHN	AVON	MARRY	DOGBERRY

Much Ado About Nothing

DUCATS	WOO	PEDRO	INSULTS	BLANK
FAINTS	HUSBAND	FRIAR	LAMENT	DENOUNCES
ORANGE	DOGBERRY	FREE SPACE	AVON	JOHN
DIED	BEATRICE	BALTHASAR	VERGES	DUEL
ANTONIO	BORACHIO	MESSINA	SONNET	LEONATO

Much Ado About Nothing

MARGARET	ORANGE	WIFE	BALTHASAR	AVON
HERO	BORACHIO	COMIC	BENEDICK	CLAUDIO
WOO	INSULTS	FREE SPACE	ANTONIO	KILL
DENOUNCES	HUSBAND	DOGBERRY	PEDRO	SONNET
MESSINA	LEONATO	LAMENT	MARRY	VERGES

Much Ado About Nothing

TOOTHACHE	FAINTS	PARTY	BLANK	CONRAD
DUEL	JOHN	LOVE	FRIAR	DUCATS
BEATRICE	VERGES	FREE SPACE	LAMENT	LEONATO
MESSINA	SONNET	PEDRO	DOGBERRY	HUSBAND
DENOUNCES	KILL	ANTONIO	DIED	INSULTS

Much Ado About Nothing

WIFE	BENEDICK	SONNET	INSULTS	BORACHIO
PEDRO	BEATRICE	VERGES	TOOTHACHE	LEONATO
DOGBERRY	WOO	FREE SPACE	HUSBAND	KILL
BLANK	CONRAD	FRIAR	MARRY	MARGARET
BALTHASAR	DENOUNCES	ANTONIO	AVON	DIED

Much Ado About Nothing

FAINTS	CLAUDIO	LAMENT	JOHN	MESSINA
PARTY	DUEL	LOVE	DUCATS	HERO
ORANGE	DIED	FREE SPACE	ANTONIO	DENOUNCES
BALTHASAR	MARGARET	MARRY	FRIAR	CONRAD
BLANK	KILL	HUSBAND	COMIC	WOO

Much Ado About Nothing

COMIC	INSULTS	DENOUNCES	HUSBAND	LOVE
BENEDICK	CLAUDIO	MARRY	FRIAR	TOOTHACHE
PEDRO	DUEL	FREE SPACE	CONRAD	KILL
BEATRICE	BLANK	LAMENT	WOO	VERGES
PARTY	ANTONIO	LEONATO	WIFE	SONNET

Much Ado About Nothing

HERO	AVON	MARGARET	BORACHIO	MESSINA
DOGBERRY	ORANGE	DUCATS	JOHN	FAINTS
BALTHASAR	SONNET	FREE SPACE	LEONATO	ANTONIO
PARTY	VERGES	WOO	LAMENT	BLANK
BEATRICE	KILL	CONRAD	DIED	DUEL

Much Ado Vocabulary Word List

No.	Word	Clue/Definition
1.	ACCORDANT	Agreeable; compatible
2.	AGATE	Type of stone showing curved, colored bands or other markings
3.	ANGLING	Fishing with hook and line
4.	APPERTAIN	Belong as a part, right, possession, or attribute
5.	ARRAS	Wall hanging, as a tapestry
6.	BETROTHS	Promises to give in marriage
7.	BETWIXT	Between; in the middle
8.	CANKER	A fungal disease in plants or ulcer in animals; also, a variety of wildflower
9.	CAPON	Castrated male chicken
10.	CARPING	Petty fault-finding
11.	CATECHIZING	Instruction by means of question and answer
12.	CINQUEPACE	Lively dance, the steps of which were regulated by the number 5
13.	CLAMOR	Loud uproar, as from a crowd of people
14.	CODPIECE	Cover for the crotch in men's hose or tight-fitting breeches
15.	COMMODITY	Article of trade or commerce
16.	CONSTABLE	Officer of the peace having police and minor judicial functions
17.	COVERTLY	In a concealed, secret, or disguised manner
18.	COXCOMB	Vain and often foolish person
19.	COZENED	Misled by means of a petty trick or fraud; deceived
20.	CUCKOLD	Husband of an unfaithful wife
21.	CUDGELED	Struck or beat with a stick
22.	DAW	Simpleton; fool
23.	DEFILED	Made filthy or dirty; unclean
24.	DISDAINED	Regarded or treated with haughty contempt; despised
25.	DISPARAGE	Speak of or treat slightingly; depreciate; belittle
26.	DISSEMBLER	One who gives a false or misleading appearance
27.	DISSUADE	Advise or urge against
28.	DOTE	Bestow or express excessive love or fondness habitually
29.	DOUBLET	Close-fitting outer garment worn by men in the Renaissance
30.	ENFRANCHISED	Freed, as from bondage
31.	ENIGMATICAL	Perplexing; mysterious
32.	ENSUING	Following as a consequence or result
33.	EPITHET	Word or phrase applied to a person to describe an actual or attributed quality
34.	EXPEDIENT	Fit or suitable for the purpose; proper under the circumstances
35.	FLOUTING	Showing contempt for
36.	FOILS	Fencing swords having a circular guard and thin, flexible blades
37.	FOLLIES	Acts lacking good sense, understanding, or foresight
38.	FRAY	Noisy fight
39.	GALLANTS	Fashionable young men
40.	HAGGARDS	Adult hawks captured for training
41.	HAVOC	Great destruction or devastation; ruinous damage
42.	HEARKEN	Give heed or attention to what is said; listen
43.	HITHER	To or toward this place
44.	IMPEDIMENT	Obstruction; hindrance; obstacle
45.	INCITE	Stir, encourage, or urge on; stimulate or prompt to action
46.	INFAMY	Extremely bad reputation
47.	INTERMINGLE	Mix or become mixed together
48.	KNAVE	Unprincipled, untrustworthy, or dishonest person
49.	LEAGUE	Unit of distance equal to 3.0 statute miles

Much Ado Vocabulary Word List (continued)

No. Word	Clue/Definition
50. LECHERY	Unrestrained or excessive indulgence of sexual desire
51. LIBERTINES	Those who act without moral restraint
52. LIEGE	Feudal lord entitled to allegiance and service
53. MALEFACTORS	Those who have committed a crime; criminals
54. MANIFEST	Make clear or evident to the eye or the understanding
55. MARL	Earthy mix of clay used as a fertilizer
56. MELANCHOLY	Gloomy state of mind; depression
57. MORTIFYING	Humiliating or shameful; hurting one's pride or self-respect
58. OBSTINATE	Firmly or stubbornly holding to one's purpose or opinion
59. OMINOUS	Portending evil or harm; foreboding; threatening
60. ORTHOGRAPHY	The art of writing
61. OSTENTATION	Conspicuous show or display intended to impress others
62. PERADVENTURE	By chance; with doubt or uncertainty
63. PERFUMER	One who makes or sells perfumes
64. PERJURY	Willful giving of false testimony under oath
65. PERNICIOUS	Causing harm or ruin
66. PERTURBATION	Mental disquiet, disturbance, or agitation
67. PESTILENCE	Deadly or virulent epidemic disease
68. PIETY	The quality of being devoutly religious
69. PLEACHED	Shaded or bordered with interlaced branches or vines
70. PONIARDS	Daggers typically having slender square or triangular blades
71. PRECEPTIAL	Procedural directive or rule
72. QUALM	Sudden feeling of apprehensive uneasiness
73. RECKONING	Settlement of accounts or of a score
74. REDEMPTION	Being saved from error or evil
75. RENDER	Provide; submit for inspection
76. REPROVE	Criticize or correct
77. REQUITED	Made a payment or return for
78. SCRUPLE	Very small portion or amount
79. SEDGES	Grass-like plants having solid stems, leaves in 3 vertical rows
80. SEMBLANCE	Outward aspect or appearance
81. SEXTON	Person employed to take care of a church
82. SHREWD	Sharp or ill-tempered
83. SIEVE	Perforated utensil used for straining or sifting
84. SLANDERED	Made false and malicious statements or reports about someone
85. SQUARER	Swashbuckler; one who delights in fighting
86. TABOR	Small drum
87. TARTLY	Sharply; in a cutting manner
88. TEDIOUS	Boring, tiring, monotonous, dull
89. THWARTING	Opposing and defeating the efforts, plans or ambitions of
90. TRAVAIL	Painfully difficult or burdensome work; toil
91. TURNCOAT	Person who changes to an opposing idea or reverses principles
92. VALOR	Boldness or determination in facing great danger
93. VARLET	Rascal; a knave
94. VICTUAL	Food supply; provisions
95. VOUCHSAFE	Allow or permit, as by favor or graciousness
96. WANTON	Sexually lawless or unrestrained

Much Ado Vocabulary Fill in the Blanks 1

_____ 1. Belong as a part, right, possession, or attribute

_____ 2. Fashionable young men

_____ 3. Fishing with hook and line

_____ 4. Showing contempt for

_____ 5. Stir, encourage, or urge on; stimulate or prompt to action

_____ 6. Noisy fight

_____ 7. Officer of the peace having police and minor judicial functions

_____ 8. Agreeable; compatible

_____ 9. The art of writing

_____ 10. Acts lacking good sense, understanding, or foresight

_____ 11. Portending evil or harm; foreboding; threatening

_____ 12. Unit of distance equal to 3.0 statute miles

_____ 13. Simpleton; fool

_____ 14. Allow or permit, as by favor or graciousness

_____ 15. Daggers typically having slender square or triangular blades

_____ 16. Earthy mix of clay used as a fertilizer

_____ 17. Obstruction; hindrance; obstacle

_____ 18. Boring, tiring, monotonous, dull

_____ 19. Conspicuous show or display intended to impress others

_____ 20. Type of stone showing curved, colored bands or other markings

Much Ado Vocabulary Fill in the Blanks 1 Answer Key

APPERTAIN	1. Belong as a part, right, possession, or attribute
GALLANTS	2. Fashionable young men
ANGLING	3. Fishing with hook and line
FLOUTING	4. Showing contempt for
INCITE	5. Stir, encourage, or urge on; stimulate or prompt to action
FRAY	6. Noisy fight
CONSTABLE	7. Officer of the peace having police and minor judicial functions
ACCORDANT	8. Agreeable; compatible
ORTHOGRAPHY	9. The art of writing
FOLLIES	10. Acts lacking good sense, understanding, or foresight
OMINOUS	11. Portending evil or harm; foreboding; threatening
LEAGUE	12. Unit of distance equal to 3.0 statute miles
DAW	13. Simpleton; fool
VOUCHSAFE	14. Allow or permit, as by favor or graciousness
PONIARDS	15. Daggers typically having slender square or triangular blades
MARL	16. Earthy mix of clay used as a fertilizer
IMPEDIMENT	17. Obstruction; hindrance; obstacle
TEDIOUS	18. Boring, tiring, monotonous, dull
OSTENTATION	19. Conspicuous show or display intended to impress others
AGATE	20. Type of stone showing curved, colored bands or other markings

Much Ado Vocabulary Fill in the Blanks 2

_____ 1. Showing contempt for

_____ 2. Made filthy or dirty; unclean

_____ 3. Struck or beat with a stick

_____ 4. Mental disquiet, disturbance, or agitation

_____ 5. In a concealed, secret, or disguised manner

_____ 6. Conspicuous show or display intended to impress others

_____ 7. Causing harm or ruin

_____ 8. Small drum

_____ 9. Boldness or determination in facing great danger

_____ 10. Mix or become mixed together

_____ 11. Portending evil or harm; foreboding; threatening

_____ 12. A fungal disease in plants or ulcer in animals; also, a variety of wildflower

_____ 13. Very small portion or amount

_____ 14. Being saved from error or evil

_____ 15. Vain and often foolish person

_____ 16. Sharp or ill-tempered

_____ 17. Obstruction; hindrance; obstacle

_____ 18. Extremely bad reputation

_____ 19. Stir, encourage, or urge on; stimulate or prompt to action

_____ 20. Adult hawks captured for training

Much Ado Vocabulary Fill in the Blanks 2 Answer Key

FLOUTING	1. Showing contempt for
DEFILED	2. Made filthy or dirty; unclean
CUDGELED	3. Struck or beat with a stick
PERTURBATION	4. Mental disquiet, disturbance, or agitation
COVERTLY	5. In a concealed, secret, or disguised manner
OSTENTATION	6. Conspicuous show or display intended to impress others
PERNICIOUS	7. Causing harm or ruin
TABOR	8. Small drum
VALOR	9. Boldness or determination in facing great danger
INTERMINGLE	10. Mix or become mixed together
OMINOUS	11. Portending evil or harm; foreboding; threatening
CANKER	12. A fungal disease in plants or ulcer in animals; also, a variety of wildflower
SCRUPLE	13. Very small portion or amount
REDEMPTION	14. Being saved from error or evil
COXCOMB	15. Vain and often foolish person
SHREWD	16. Sharp or ill-tempered
IMPEDIMENT	17. Obstruction; hindrance; obstacle
INFAMY	18. Extremely bad reputation
INCITE	19. Stir, encourage, or urge on; stimulate or prompt to action
HAGGARDS	20. Adult hawks captured for training

Much Ado Vocabulary Fill in the Blanks 3

1. Portending evil or harm; foreboding; threatening
2. Word or phrase applied to a person to describe an actual or attributed quality
3. Shaded or bordered with interlaced branches or vines
4. Perplexing; mysterious
5. Made filthy or dirty; unclean
6. Those who act without moral restraint
7. Small drum
8. Unit of distance equal to 3.0 statute miles
9. Daggers typically having slender square or triangular blades
10. Conspicuous show or display intended to impress others
11. Unprincipled, untrustworthy, or dishonest person
12. Person employed to take care of a church
13. Sexually lawless or unrestrained
14. Struck or beat with a stick
15. By chance; with doubt or uncertainty
16. Following as a consequence or result
17. Simpleton; fool
18. Misled by means of a petty trick or fraud; deceived
19. Husband of an unfaithful wife
20. Grass-like plants having solid stems, leaves in 3 vertical rows

Much Ado Vocabulary Fill in the Blanks 3 Answer Key

OMINOUS	1. Portending evil or harm; foreboding; threatening
EPITHET	2. Word or phrase applied to a person to describe an actual or attributed quality
PLEACHED	3. Shaded or bordered with interlaced branches or vines
ENIGMATICAL	4. Perplexing; mysterious
DEFILED	5. Made filthy or dirty; unclean
LIBERTINES	6. Those who act without moral restraint
TABOR	7. Small drum
LEAGUE	8. Unit of distance equal to 3.0 statute miles
PONIARDS	9. Daggers typically having slender square or triangular blades
OSTENTATION	10. Conspicuous show or display intended to impress others
KNAVE	11. Unprincipled, untrustworthy, or dishonest person
SEXTON	12. Person employed to take care of a church
WANTON	13. Sexually lawless or unrestrained
CUDGELED	14. Struck or beat with a stick
PERADVENTURE	15. By chance; with doubt or uncertainty
ENSUING	16. Following as a consequence or result
DAW	17. Simpleton; fool
COZENED	18. Misled by means of a petty trick or fraud; deceived
CUCKOLD	19. Husband of an unfaithful wife
SEDGES	20. Grass-like plants having solid stems, leaves in 3 vertical rows

Much Ado Vocabulary Fill in the Blanks 4

1. Made a payment or return for
2. Person employed to take care of a church
3. Speak of or treat slightingly; depreciate; belittle
4. Causing harm or ruin
5. Small drum
6. Shaded or bordered with interlaced branches or vines
7. Gloomy state of mind; depression
8. Fencing swords having a circular guard and thin, flexible blades
9. The art of writing
10. Criticize or correct
11. Misled by means of a petty trick or fraud; deceived
12. Feudal lord entitled to allegiance and service
13. Firmly or stubbornly holding to one's purpose or opinion
14. Word or phrase applied to a person to describe an actual or attributed quality
15. Sharp or ill-tempered
16. Belong as a part, right, possession, or attribute
17. Obstruction; hindrance; obstacle
18. Fashionable young men
19. Adult hawks captured for training
20. By chance; with doubt or uncertainty

Much Ado Vocabulary Fill in the Blanks 4 Answer Key

REQUITED	1. Made a payment or return for
SEXTON	2. Person employed to take care of a church
DISPARAGE	3. Speak of or treat slightingly; depreciate; belittle
PERNICIOUS	4. Causing harm or ruin
TABOR	5. Small drum
PLEACHED	6. Shaded or bordered with interlaced branches or vines
MELANCHOLY	7. Gloomy state of mind; depression
FOILS	8. Fencing swords having a circular guard and thin, flexible blades
ORTHOGRAPHY	9. The art of writing
REPROVE	10. Criticize or correct
COZENED	11. Misled by means of a petty trick or fraud; deceived
LIEGE	12. Feudal lord entitled to allegiance and service
OBSTINATE	13. Firmly or stubbornly holding to one's purpose or opinion
EPITHET	14. Word or phrase applied to a person to describe an actual or attributed quality
SHREWD	15. Sharp or ill-tempered
APPERTAIN	16. Belong as a part, right, possession, or attribute
IMPEDIMENT	17. Obstruction; hindrance; obstacle
GALLANTS	18. Fashionable young men
HAGGARDS	19. Adult hawks captured for training
PERADVENTURE	20. By chance; with doubt or uncertainty

Much Ado Vocabulary Matching 1

___ 1. PONIARDS   A. Wall hanging, as a tapestry
___ 2. GALLANTS   B. Humiliating or shameful; hurting one's pride or self-respect
___ 3. DAW   C. Person employed to take care of a church
___ 4. CUCKOLD   D. Perplexing; mysterious
___ 5. COMMODITY   E. Made false and malicious statements or reports about someone
___ 6. MARL   F. Grass-like plants having solid stems, leaves in 3 vertical rows
___ 7. MORTIFYING   G. Husband of an unfaithful wife
___ 8. TRAVAIL   H. Outward aspect or appearance
___ 9. SLANDERED   I. Simpleton; fool
___10. SEXTON   J. Boldness or determination in facing great danger
___11. SEDGES   K. Fashionable young men
___12. MELANCHOLY   L. A fungal disease in plants or ulcer in animals; also, a variety of wildflower
___13. DISSEMBLER   M. One who gives a false or misleading appearance
___14. OMINOUS   N. Earthy mix of clay used as a fertilizer
___15. ENIGMATICAL   O. Make clear or evident to the eye or the understanding
___16. ENSUING   P. Close-fitting outer garment worn by men in the Renaissance
___17. DOUBLET   Q. To or toward this place
___18. HITHER   R. Article of trade or commerce
___19. PESTILENCE   S. Deadly or virulent epidemic disease
___20. SQUARER   T. Portending evil or harm; foreboding; threatening
___21. CANKER   U. Swashbuckler; one who delights in fighting
___22. SEMBLANCE   V. Gloomy state of mind; depression
___23. ARRAS   W. Painfully difficult or burdensome work; toil
___24. VALOR   X. Daggers typically having slender square or triangular blades
___25. MANIFEST   Y. Following as a consequence or result

Much Ado Vocabulary Matching 1 Answer Key

X - 1. PONIARDS	A.	Wall hanging, as a tapestry
K - 2. GALLANTS	B.	Humiliating or shameful; hurting one's pride or self-respect
I - 3. DAW	C.	Person employed to take care of a church
G - 4. CUCKOLD	D.	Perplexing; mysterious
R - 5. COMMODITY	E.	Made false and malicious statements or reports about someone
N - 6. MARL	F.	Grass-like plants having solid stems, leaves in 3 vertical rows
B - 7. MORTIFYING	G.	Husband of an unfaithful wife
W - 8. TRAVAIL	H.	Outward aspect or appearance
E - 9. SLANDERED	I.	Simpleton; fool
C - 10. SEXTON	J.	Boldness or determination in facing great danger
F - 11. SEDGES	K.	Fashionable young men
V - 12. MELANCHOLY	L.	A fungal disease in plants or ulcer in animals; also, a variety of wildflower
M - 13. DISSEMBLER	M.	One who gives a false or misleading appearance
T - 14. OMINOUS	N.	Earthy mix of clay used as a fertilizer
D - 15. ENIGMATICAL	O.	Make clear or evident to the eye or the understanding
Y - 16. ENSUING	P.	Close-fitting outer garment worn by men in the Renaissance
P - 17. DOUBLET	Q.	To or toward this place
Q - 18. HITHER	R.	Article of trade or commerce
S - 19. PESTILENCE	S.	Deadly or virulent epidemic disease
U - 20. SQUARER	T.	Portending evil or harm; foreboding; threatening
L - 21. CANKER	U.	Swashbuckler; one who delights in fighting
H - 22. SEMBLANCE	V.	Gloomy state of mind; depression
A - 23. ARRAS	W.	Painfully difficult or burdensome work; toil
J - 24. VALOR	X.	Daggers typically having slender square or triangular blades
O - 25. MANIFEST	Y.	Following as a consequence or result

Much Ado Vocabulary Matching 2

___ 1. MORTIFYING
___ 2. PIETY
___ 3. DEFILED
___ 4. SLANDERED
___ 5. DISDAINED
___ 6. PERJURY
___ 7. VALOR
___ 8. SCRUPLE
___ 9. APPERTAIN
___ 10. MANIFEST
___ 11. COVERTLY
___ 12. WANTON
___ 13. RENDER
___ 14. PERFUMER
___ 15. RECKONING
___ 16. SEXTON
___ 17. SIEVE
___ 18. PERTURBATION
___ 19. BETWIXT
___ 20. CUCKOLD
___ 21. PESTILENCE
___ 22. CODPIECE
___ 23. COXCOMB
___ 24. EXPEDIENT
___ 25. CLAMOR

A. Cover for the crotch in men's hose or tight-fitting breeches
B. Regarded or treated with haughty contempt; despised
C. Perforated utensil used for straining or sifting
D. Make clear or evident to the eye or the understanding
E. Vain and often foolish person
F. Person employed to take care of a church
G. Made filthy or dirty; unclean
H. Fit or suitable for the purpose; proper under the circumstances
I. Humiliating or shameful; hurting one's pride or self-respect
J. Provide; submit for inspection
K. Loud uproar, as from a crowd of people
L. Deadly or virulent epidemic disease
M. Made false and malicious statements or reports about someone
N. Settlement of accounts or of a score
O. Husband of an unfaithful wife
P. One who makes or sells perfumes
Q. Between; in the middle
R. Sexually lawless or unrestrained
S. Boldness or determination in facing great danger
T. Mental disquiet, disturbance, or agitation
U. Very small portion or amount
V. The quality of being devoutly religious
W. Belong as a part, right, possession, or attribute
X. Willful giving of false testimony under oath
Y. In a concealed, secret, or disguised manner

Much Ado Vocabulary Matching 2 Answer Key

I - 1. MORTIFYING	A.	Cover for the crotch in men's hose or tight-fitting breeches
V - 2. PIETY	B.	Regarded or treated with haughty contempt; despised
G - 3. DEFILED	C.	Perforated utensil used for straining or sifting
M - 4. SLANDERED	D.	Make clear or evident to the eye or the understanding
B - 5. DISDAINED	E.	Vain and often foolish person
X - 6. PERJURY	F.	Person employed to take care of a church
S - 7. VALOR	G.	Made filthy or dirty; unclean
U - 8. SCRUPLE	H.	Fit or suitable for the purpose; proper under the circumstances
W - 9. APPERTAIN	I.	Humiliating or shameful; hurting one's pride or self-respect
D - 10. MANIFEST	J.	Provide; submit for inspection
Y - 11. COVERTLY	K.	Loud uproar, as from a crowd of people
R - 12. WANTON	L.	Deadly or virulent epidemic disease
J - 13. RENDER	M.	Made false and malicious statements or reports about someone
P - 14. PERFUMER	N.	Settlement of accounts or of a score
N - 15. RECKONING	O.	Husband of an unfaithful wife
F - 16. SEXTON	P.	One who makes or sells perfumes
C - 17. SIEVE	Q.	Between; in the middle
T - 18. PERTURBATION	R.	Sexually lawless or unrestrained
Q - 19. BETWIXT	S.	Boldness or determination in facing great danger
O - 20. CUCKOLD	T.	Mental disquiet, disturbance, or agitation
L - 21. PESTILENCE	U.	Very small portion or amount
A - 22. CODPIECE	V.	The quality of being devoutly religious
E - 23. COXCOMB	W.	Belong as a part, right, possession, or attribute
H - 24. EXPEDIENT	X.	Willful giving of false testimony under oath
K - 25. CLAMOR	Y.	In a concealed, secret, or disguised manner

Much Ado Vocabulary Matching 3

___ 1. MANIFEST
___ 2. SCRUPLE
___ 3. SEMBLANCE
___ 4. CONSTABLE
___ 5. OSTENTATION
___ 6. CINQUEPACE
___ 7. QUALM
___ 8. DOUBLET
___ 9. RECKONING
___ 10. ENIGMATICAL
___ 11. EXPEDIENT
___ 12. THWARTING
___ 13. SIEVE
___ 14. TEDIOUS
___ 15. REDEMPTION
___ 16. FOLLIES
___ 17. ENFRANCHISED
___ 18. FOILS
___ 19. DISPARAGE
___ 20. TURNCOAT
___ 21. TRAVAIL
___ 22. INTERMINGLE
___ 23. DAW
___ 24. OMINOUS
___ 25. MORTIFYING

A. Person who changes to an opposing idea or reverses principles
B. Fencing swords having a circular guard and thin, flexible blades
C. Being saved from error or evil
D. Sudden feeling of apprehensive uneasiness
E. Boring, tiring, monotonous, dull
F. Simpleton; fool
G. Speak of or treat slightingly; depreciate; belittle
H. Very small portion or amount
I. Freed, as from bondage
J. Officer of the peace having police and minor judicial functions
K. Fit or suitable for the purpose; proper under the circumstances
L. Make clear or evident to the eye or the understanding
M. Close-fitting outer garment worn by men in the Renaissance
N. Perforated utensil used for straining or sifting
O. Outward aspect or appearance
P. Acts lacking good sense, understanding, or foresight
Q. Conspicuous show or display intended to impress others
R. Lively dance, the steps of which were regulated by the number 5
S. Perplexing; mysterious
T. Settlement of accounts or of a score
U. Humiliating or shameful; hurting one's pride or self-respect
V. Painfully difficult or burdensome work; toil
W. Mix or become mixed together
X. Portending evil or harm; foreboding; threatening
Y. Opposing and defeating the efforts, plans or ambitions of

Much Ado Vocabulary Matching 3 Answer Key

L - 1.	MANIFEST	A. Person who changes to an opposing idea or reverses principles
H - 2.	SCRUPLE	B. Fencing swords having a circular guard and thin, flexible blades
O - 3.	SEMBLANCE	C. Being saved from error or evil
J - 4.	CONSTABLE	D. Sudden feeling of apprehensive uneasiness
Q - 5.	OSTENTATION	E. Boring, tiring, monotonous, dull
R - 6.	CINQUEPACE	F. Simpleton; fool
D - 7.	QUALM	G. Speak of or treat slightingly; depreciate; belittle
M - 8.	DOUBLET	H. Very small portion or amount
T - 9.	RECKONING	I. Freed, as from bondage
S - 10.	ENIGMATICAL	J. Officer of the peace having police and minor judicial functions
K - 11.	EXPEDIENT	K. Fit or suitable for the purpose; proper under the circumstances
Y - 12.	THWARTING	L. Make clear or evident to the eye or the understanding
N - 13.	SIEVE	M. Close-fitting outer garment worn by men in the Renaissance
E - 14.	TEDIOUS	N. Perforated utensil used for straining or sifting
C - 15.	REDEMPTION	O. Outward aspect or appearance
P - 16.	FOLLIES	P. Acts lacking good sense, understanding, or foresight
I - 17.	ENFRANCHISED	Q. Conspicuous show or display intended to impress others
B - 18.	FOILS	R. Lively dance, the steps of which were regulated by the number 5
G - 19.	DISPARAGE	S. Perplexing; mysterious
A - 20.	TURNCOAT	T. Settlement of accounts or of a score
V - 21.	TRAVAIL	U. Humiliating or shameful; hurting one's pride or self-respect
W - 22.	INTERMINGLE	V. Painfully difficult or burdensome work; toil
F - 23.	DAW	W. Mix or become mixed together
X - 24.	OMINOUS	X. Portending evil or harm; foreboding; threatening
U - 25.	MORTIFYING	Y. Opposing and defeating the efforts, plans or ambitions of

Much Ado Vocabulary Matching 4

___ 1. LIBERTINES
___ 2. ORTHOGRAPHY
___ 3. DISSEMBLER
___ 4. SEXTON
___ 5. FOILS
___ 6. PESTILENCE
___ 7. DOUBLET
___ 8. RECKONING
___ 9. DISPARAGE
___ 10. INTERMINGLE
___ 11. IMPEDIMENT
___ 12. EPITHET
___ 13. REDEMPTION
___ 14. VALOR
___ 15. HITHER
___ 16. CODPIECE
___ 17. MALEFACTORS
___ 18. VOUCHSAFE
___ 19. ACCORDANT
___ 20. DOTE
___ 21. ANGLING
___ 22. COVERTLY
___ 23. OSTENTATION
___ 24. PONIARDS
___ 25. DISDAINED

A. Obstruction; hindrance; obstacle
B. Close-fitting outer garment worn by men in the Renaissance
C. Those who act without moral restraint
D. Fencing swords having a circular guard and thin, flexible blades
E. Settlement of accounts or of a score
F. Deadly or virulent epidemic disease
G. Agreeable; compatible
H. In a concealed, secret, or disguised manner
I. Mix or become mixed together
J. Fishing with hook and line
K. Bestow or express excessive love or fondness habitually
L. Person employed to take care of a church
M. Conspicuous show or display intended to impress others
N. Boldness or determination in facing great danger
O. Cover for the crotch in men's hose or tight-fitting breeches
P. Regarded or treated with haughty contempt; despised
Q. One who gives a false or misleading appearance
R. Word or phrase applied to a person to describe an actual or attributed quality
S. Allow or permit, as by favor or graciousness
T. The art of writing
U. Being saved from error or evil
V. To or toward this place
W. Those who have committed a crime; criminals
X. Speak of or treat slightingly; depreciate; belittle
Y. Daggers typically having slender square or triangular blades

Much Ado Vocabulary Matching 4 Answer Key

C - 1.	LIBERTINES	A. Obstruction; hindrance; obstacle
T - 2.	ORTHOGRAPHY	B. Close-fitting outer garment worn by men in the Renaissance
Q - 3.	DISSEMBLER	C. Those who act without moral restraint
L - 4.	SEXTON	D. Fencing swords having a circular guard and thin, flexible blades
D - 5.	FOILS	E. Settlement of accounts or of a score
F - 6.	PESTILENCE	F. Deadly or virulent epidemic disease
B - 7.	DOUBLET	G. Agreeable; compatible
E - 8.	RECKONING	H. In a concealed, secret, or disguised manner
X - 9.	DISPARAGE	I. Mix or become mixed together
I - 10.	INTERMINGLE	J. Fishing with hook and line
A - 11.	IMPEDIMENT	K. Bestow or express excessive love or fondness habitually
R - 12.	EPITHET	L. Person employed to take care of a church
U - 13.	REDEMPTION	M. Conspicuous show or display intended to impress others
N - 14.	VALOR	N. Boldness or determination in facing great danger
V - 15.	HITHER	O. Cover for the crotch in men's hose or tight-fitting breeches
O - 16.	CODPIECE	P. Regarded or treated with haughty contempt; despised
W - 17.	MALEFACTORS	Q. One who gives a false or misleading appearance
S - 18.	VOUCHSAFE	R. Word or phrase applied to a person to describe an actual or attributed quality
G - 19.	ACCORDANT	S. Allow or permit, as by favor or graciousness
K - 20.	DOTE	T. The art of writing
J - 21.	ANGLING	U. Being saved from error or evil
H - 22.	COVERTLY	V. To or toward this place
M - 23.	OSTENTATION	W. Those who have committed a crime; criminals
Y - 24.	PONIARDS	X. Speak of or treat slightingly; depreciate; belittle
P - 25.	DISDAINED	Y. Daggers typically having slender square or triangular blades

Much Ado Vocabulary Magic Squares 1

Match the definition with the vocabulary word. Put your answers in the magic squares below. When your answers are correct, all columns and rows will add to the same number.

A. FRAY
B. IMPEDIMENT
C. SEMBLANCE
D. VOUCHSAFE
E. MORTIFYING
F. RENDER
G. AGATE
H. VICTUAL
I. CLAMOR
J. REPROVE
K. OSTENTATION
L. FOILS
M. BETWIXT
N. PONIARDS
O. SLANDERED
P. EXPEDIENT

1. Provide; submit for inspection
2. Loud uproar, as from a crowd of people
3. Made false and malicious statements or reports about someone
4. Allow or permit, as by favor or graciousness
5. Between; in the middle
6. Obstruction; hindrance; obstacle
7. Food supply; provisions
8. Conspicuous show or display intended to impress others
9. Outward aspect or appearance
10. Fit or suitable for the purpose; proper under the circumstances
11. Criticize or correct
12. Humiliating or shameful; hurting one's pride or self-respect
13. Fencing swords having a circular guard and thin, flexible blades
14. Type of stone showing curved, colored bands or other markings
15. Noisy fight
16. Daggers typically having slender square or triangular blades

A=	B=	C=	D=
E=	F=	G=	H=
I=	J=	K=	L=
M=	N=	O=	P=

Much Ado Vocabulary Magic Squares 1 Answer Key

Match the definition with the vocabulary word. Put your answers in the magic squares below. When your answers are correct, all columns and rows will add to the same number.

A. FRAY
B. IMPEDIMENT
C. SEMBLANCE
D. VOUCHSAFE
E. MORTIFYING
F. RENDER
G. AGATE
H. VICTUAL
I. CLAMOR
J. REPROVE
K. OSTENTATION
L. FOILS
M. BETWIXT
N. PONIARDS
O. SLANDERED
P. EXPEDIENT

1. Provide; submit for inspection
2. Loud uproar, as from a crowd of people
3. Made false and malicious statements or reports about someone
4. Allow or permit, as by favor or graciousness
5. Between; in the middle
6. Obstruction; hindrance; obstacle
7. Food supply; provisions
8. Conspicuous show or display intended to impress others
9. Outward aspect or appearance
10. Fit or suitable for the purpose; proper under the circumstances
11. Criticize or correct
12. Humiliating or shameful; hurting one's pride or self-respect
13. Fencing swords having a circular guard and thin, flexible blades
14. Type of stone showing curved, colored bands or other markings
15. Noisy fight
16. Daggers typically having slender square or triangular blades

A=15	B=6	C=9	D=4
E=12	F=1	G=14	H=7
I=2	J=11	K=8	L=13
M=5	N=16	O=3	P=10

Much Ado Vocabulary Magic Squares 2

Match the definition with the vocabulary word. Put your answers in the magic squares below. When your answers are correct, all columns and rows will add to the same number.

A. THWARTING
B. RENDER
C. DISSEMBLER
D. OBSTINATE
E. OMINOUS
F. PERADVENTURE
G. VICTUAL
H. AGATE
I. IMPEDIMENT
J. CUDGELED
K. INCITE
L. CINQUEPACE
M. COVERTLY
N. PERNICIOUS
O. VARLET
P. ANGLING

1. Rascal; a knave
2. Struck or beat with a stick
3. Type of stone showing curved, colored bands or other markings
4. Opposing and defeating the efforts, plans or ambitions of
5. Firmly or stubbornly holding to one's purpose or opinion
6. Portending evil or harm; foreboding; threatening
7. Stir, encourage, or urge on; stimulate or prompt to action
8. Causing harm or ruin
9. By chance; with doubt or uncertainty
10. One who gives a false or misleading appearance
11. In a concealed, secret, or disguised manner
12. Lively dance, the steps of which were regulated by the number 5
13. Obstruction; hindrance; obstacle
14. Fishing with hook and line
15. Provide; submit for inspection
16. Food supply; provisions

A=	B=	C=	D=
E=	F=	G=	H=
I=	J=	K=	L=
M=	N=	O=	P=

Much Ado Vocabulary Magic Squares 2 Answer Key

Match the definition with the vocabulary word. Put your answers in the magic squares below. When your answers are correct, all columns and rows will add to the same number.

A. THWARTING
B. RENDER
C. DISSEMBLER
D. OBSTINATE
E. OMINOUS
F. PERADVENTURE

G. VICTUAL
H. AGATE
I. IMPEDIMENT
J. CUDGELED
K. INCITE
L. CINQUEPACE

M. COVERTLY
N. PERNICIOUS
O. VARLET
P. ANGLING

1. Rascal; a knave
2. Struck or beat with a stick
3. Type of stone showing curved, colored bands or other markings
4. Opposing and defeating the efforts, plans or ambitions of
5. Firmly or stubbornly holding to one's purpose or opinion
6. Portending evil or harm; foreboding; threatening
7. Stir, encourage, or urge on; stimulate or prompt to action
8. Causing harm or ruin
9. By chance; with doubt or uncertainty
10. One who gives a false or misleading appearance
11. In a concealed, secret, or disguised manner
12. Lively dance, the steps of which were regulated by the number 5
13. Obstruction; hindrance; obstacle
14. Fishing with hook and line
15. Provide; submit for inspection
16. Food supply; provisions

A=4	B=15	C=10	D=5
E=6	F=9	G=16	H=3
I=13	J=2	K=7	L=12
M=11	N=8	O=1	P=14

Much Ado Vocabulary Magic Squares 3

Match the definition with the vocabulary word. Put your answers in the magic squares below. When your answers are correct, all columns and rows will add to the same number.

A. LIBERTINES
B. SLANDERED
C. DAW
D. PRECEPTIAL
E. DOTE
F. BETROTHS
G. INFAMY
H. MARL
I. INTERMINGLE
J. KNAVE
K. LECHERY
L. DEFILED
M. DISDAINED
N. SEMBLANCE
O. PERTURBATION
P. MELANCHOLY

1. Earthy mix of clay used as a fertilizer
2. Regarded or treated with haughty contempt; despised
3. Made false and malicious statements or reports about someone
4. Unrestrained or excessive indulgence of sexual desire
5. Unprincipled, untrustworthy, or dishonest person
6. Simpleton; fool
7. Gloomy state of mind; depression
8. Bestow or express excessive love or fondness habitually
9. Mental disquiet, disturbance, or agitation
10. Promises to give in marriage
11. Mix or become mixed together
12. Procedural directive or rule
13. Those who act without moral restraint
14. Made filthy or dirty; unclean
15. Extremely bad reputation
16. Outward aspect or appearance

A=	B=	C=	D=
E=	F=	G=	H=
I=	J=	K=	L=
M=	N=	O=	P=

Much Ado Vocabulary Magic Squares 3 Answer Key

Match the definition with the vocabulary word. Put your answers in the magic squares below. When your answers are correct, all columns and rows will add to the same number.

A. LIBERTINES
B. SLANDERED
C. DAW
D. PRECEPTIAL
E. DOTE
F. BETROTHS
G. INFAMY
H. MARL
I. INTERMINGLE
J. KNAVE
K. LECHERY
L. DEFILED
M. DISDAINED
N. SEMBLANCE
O. PERTURBATION
P. MELANCHOLY

1. Earthy mix of clay used as a fertilizer
2. Regarded or treated with haughty contempt; despised
3. Made false and malicious statements or reports about someone
4. Unrestrained or excessive indulgence of sexual desire
5. Unprincipled, untrustworthy, or dishonest person
6. Simpleton; fool
7. Gloomy state of mind; depression
8. Bestow or express excessive love or fondness habitually
9. Mental disquiet, disturbance, or agitation
10. Promises to give in marriage
11. Mix or become mixed together
12. Procedural directive or rule
13. Those who act without moral restraint
14. Made filthy or dirty; unclean
15. Extremely bad reputation
16. Outward aspect or appearance

A=13	B=3	C=6	D=12
E=8	F=10	G=15	H=1
I=11	J=5	K=4	L=14
M=2	N=16	O=9	P=7

Much Ado Vocabulary Magic Squares 4

Match the definition with the vocabulary word. Put your answers in the magic squares below. When your answers are correct, all columns and rows will add to the same number.

A. TEDIOUS
B. CANKER
C. INCITE
D. DEFILED
E. VARLET
F. RECKONING
G. EPITHET
H. OBSTINATE
I. MELANCHOLY
J. GALLANTS
K. DOUBLET
L. SLANDERED
M. AGATE
N. WANTON
O. TARTLY
P. PESTILENCE

1. Type of stone showing curved, colored bands or other markings
2. Settlement of accounts or of a score
3. Firmly or stubbornly holding to one's purpose or opinion
4. Sharply; in a cutting manner
5. Made false and malicious statements or reports about someone
6. Stir, encourage, or urge on; stimulate or prompt to action
7. Boring, tiring, monotonous, dull
8. Fashionable young men
9. Close-fitting outer garment worn by men in the Renaissance
10. Made filthy or dirty; unclean
11. A fungal disease in plants or ulcer in animals; also, a variety of wildflower
12. Gloomy state of mind; depression
13. Sexually lawless or unrestrained
14. Rascal; a knave
15. Word or phrase applied to a person to describe an actual or attributed quality
16. Deadly or virulent epidemic disease

A=	B=	C=	D=
E=	F=	G=	H=
I=	J=	K=	L=
M=	N=	O=	P=

Much Ado Vocabulary Magic Squares 4 Answer Key

Match the definition with the vocabulary word. Put your answers in the magic squares below. When your answers are correct, all columns and rows will add to the same number.

A. TEDIOUS
B. CANKER
C. INCITE
D. DEFILED
E. VARLET
F. RECKONING
G. EPITHET
H. OBSTINATE
I. MELANCHOLY
J. GALLANTS
K. DOUBLET
L. SLANDERED
M. AGATE
N. WANTON
O. TARTLY
P. PESTILENCE

1. Type of stone showing curved, colored bands or other markings
2. Settlement of accounts or of a score
3. Firmly or stubbornly holding to one's purpose or opinion
4. Sharply; in a cutting manner
5. Made false and malicious statements or reports about someone
6. Stir, encourage, or urge on; stimulate or prompt to action
7. Boring, tiring, monotonous, dull
8. Fashionable young men
9. Close-fitting outer garment worn by men in the Renaissance
10. Made filthy or dirty; unclean
11. A fungal disease in plants or ulcer in animals; also, a variety of wildflower
12. Gloomy state of mind; depression
13. Sexually lawless or unrestrained
14. Rascal; a knave
15. Word or phrase applied to a person to describe an actual or attributed quality
16. Deadly or virulent epidemic disease

A=7	B=11	C=6	D=10
E=14	F=2	G=15	H=3
I=12	J=8	K=9	L=5
M=1	N=13	O=4	P=16

Much Ado Vocabulary Word Search 1

```
I P I E T Y C A M A N I F E S T C V
N L T L S J A P F S X L B S A V I R
F E D E R P T P R Z S I V J G A M Q
A A I C H E E E W L R E J X A L P V
M G S H A R C R K A E G V C T O E N
Y U D E V F H T Z B N E Y A E R D Q
C E A R O U I A C J D T V P R V I F
W I I Y C M Z I P A E G O O F L M C
F K N A V E I N T E R M I N G L E L
C Q E Q R R N N N F B P S C C H N T
C A D F U E G A O T Q V I E M A T S
T L N I O E P R D U E U D N D G C V
H R A K N I P R G H S D A W G G S C
X X X M E C L A O G H I I L N A E T
M A R L O R I S C V R D E O M R F S
T A B O R R R T Z E E D O V U D R R
E P I T H E T B E T W I X T E S A Q
S E X T O N D C C U D G E L E D Y Z
```

A fungal disease in plants or ulcer in animals; also, a variety of wildflower (6)
Adult hawks captured for training (8)
Belong as a part, right, possession, or attribute (9)
Bestow or express excessive love or fondness habitually (4)
Between; in the middle (7)
Boldness or determination in facing great danger (5)
Boring, tiring, monotonous, dull (7)
Castrated male chicken (5)
Criticize or correct (7)
Earthy mix of clay used as a fertilizer (4)
Extremely bad reputation (6)
Fencing swords having a circular guard and thin, flexible blades (5)
Feudal lord entitled to allegiance and service (5)
Grass-like plants having solid stems, leaves in 3 vertical rows (6)
Great destruction or devastation; ruinous damage (5)
Instruction by means of question and answer (11)
Lively dance, the steps of which were regulated by the number 5 (10)
Loud uproar, as from a crowd of people (6)
Make clear or evident to the eye or the understanding (8)
Mix or become mixed together (11)
Noisy fight (4)
Obstruction; hindrance; obstacle (10)

One who makes or sells perfumes (8)
Perforated utensil used for straining or sifting (5)
Person employed to take care of a church (6)
Petty fault-finding (7)
Portending evil or harm; foreboding; threatening (7)
Provide; submit for inspection (6)
Rascal; a knave (6)
Regarded or treated with haughty contempt; despised (9)
Sexually lawless or unrestrained (6)
Sharp or ill-tempered (6)
Simpleton; fool (3)
Small drum (5)
Stir, encourage, or urge on; stimulate or prompt to action (6)
Struck or beat with a stick (8)
Sudden feeling of apprehensive uneasiness (5)
The quality of being devoutly religious (5)
Type of stone showing curved, colored bands or other markings (5)
Unit of distance equal to 3.0 statute miles (6)
Unprincipled, untrustworthy, or dishonest person (5)
Unrestrained or excessive indulgence of sexual desire (7)
Wall hanging, as a tapestry (5)
Word or phrase applied to a person to describe an actual or attributed quality (7)

Much Ado Vocabulary Word Search 1 Answer Key

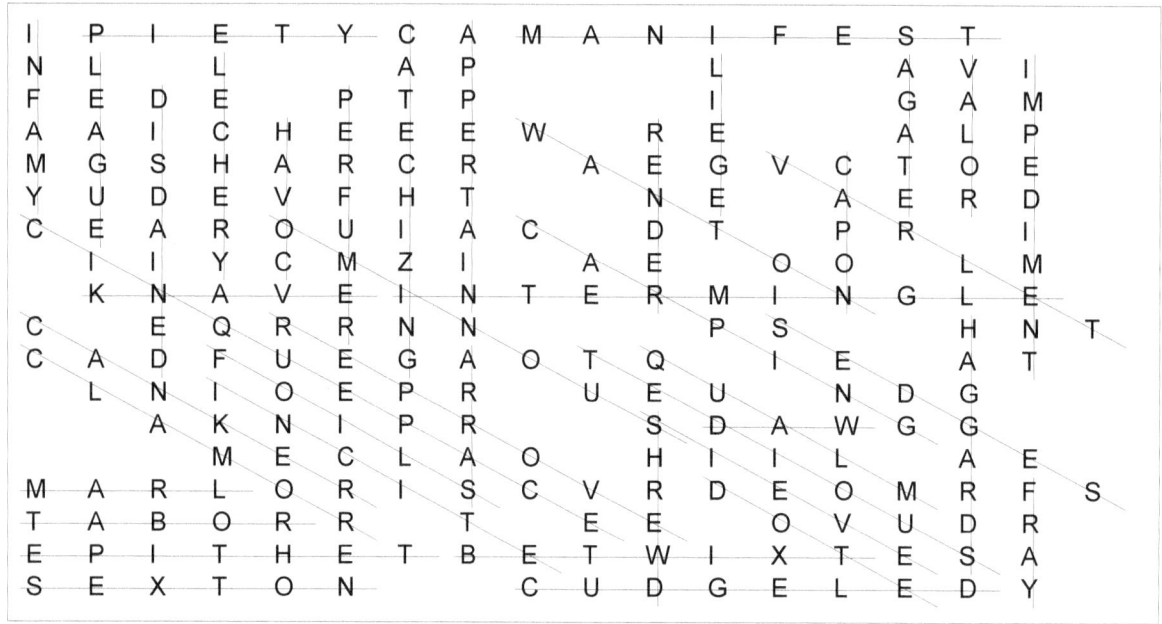

A fungal disease in plants or ulcer in animals; also, a variety of wildflower (6)
Adult hawks captured for training (8)
Belong as a part, right, possession, or attribute (9)
Bestow or express excessive love or fondness habitually (4)
Between; in the middle (7)
Boldness or determination in facing great danger (5)
Boring, tiring, monotonous, dull (7)
Castrated male chicken (5)
Criticize or correct (7)
Earthy mix of clay used as a fertilizer (4)
Extremely bad reputation (6)
Fencing swords having a circular guard and thin, flexible blades (5)
Feudal lord entitled to allegiance and service (5)
Grass-like plants having solid stems, leaves in 3 vertical rows (6)
Great destruction or devastation; ruinous damage (5)
Instruction by means of question and answer (11)
Lively dance, the steps of which were regulated by the number 5 (10)
Loud uproar, as from a crowd of people (6)
Make clear or evident to the eye or the understanding (8)
Mix or become mixed together (11)
Noisy fight (4)
Obstruction; hindrance; obstacle (10)

One who makes or sells perfumes (8)
Perforated utensil used for straining or sifting (5)
Person employed to take care of a church (6)
Petty fault-finding (7)
Portending evil or harm; foreboding; threatening (7)
Provide; submit for inspection (6)
Rascal; a knave (6)
Regarded or treated with haughty contempt; despised (9)
Sexually lawless or unrestrained (6)
Sharp or ill-tempered (6)
Simpleton; fool (3)
Small drum (5)
Stir, encourage, or urge on; stimulate or prompt to action (6)
Struck or beat with a stick (8)
Sudden feeling of apprehensive uneasiness (5)
The quality of being devoutly religious (5)
Type of stone showing curved, colored bands or other markings (5)
Unit of distance equal to 3.0 statute miles (6)
Unprincipled, untrustworthy, or dishonest person (5)
Unrestrained or excessive indulgence of sexual desire (7)
Wall hanging, as a tapestry (5)
Word or phrase applied to a person to describe an actual or attributed quality (7)

Much Ado Vocabulary Word Search 2

M	A	N	I	F	E	S	T	P	L	E	A	C	H	E	D	A	D
O	V	K	H	Y	C	I	N	S	A	H	W	F	X	P	D	C	H
R	Y	G	A	Z	O	E	Y	T	E	G	P	N	W	R	Y	C	N
T	F	G	V	G	Z	V	D	I	S	D	A	I	N	E	D	O	H
I	M	X	O	Q	E	E	E	O	T	Z	G	T	R	C	F	R	S
F	A	O	C	C	N	P	F	T	U	A	V	E	E	E	L	D	G
Y	R	A	R	A	E	Q	I	K	R	B	B	T	S	P	F	A	N
I	L	R	C	T	D	G	L	T	N	F	L	O	U	T	I	N	G
N	S	R	L	E	H	F	E	H	H	A	T	E	R	I	D	T	N
G	E	A	A	C	M	O	D	W	V	E	V	R	T	A	I	Q	H
G	M	S	M	H	V	I	G	A	Q	C	T	E	A	L	S	J	Q
A	B	M	O	I	A	L	T	R	U	O	K	Y	W	V	P	W	K
L	L	C	R	Z	L	S	P	T	A	D	D	F	C	M	A	X	B
L	A	B	Y	I	O	E	J	I	L	P	Y	R	A	D	R	I	Z
A	N	W	Z	N	R	R	A	N	M	I	H	A	N	Z	A	F	L
N	C	A	N	G	L	I	N	G	N	E	C	Y	K	L	G	W	Z
T	E	I	N	C	I	T	E	N	U	C	L	I	E	G	E	D	B
S	Q	U	A	R	E	R	J	P	I	E	T	Y	R	D	O	T	E

- A fungal disease in plants or ulcer in animals; also, a variety of wildflower (6)
- Agreeable; compatible (9)
- Bestow or express excessive love or fondness habitually (4)
- Boldness or determination in facing great danger (5)
- Close-fitting outer garment worn by men in the Renaissance (7)
- Cover for the crotch in men's hose or tight-fitting breeches (8)
- Earthy mix of clay used as a fertilizer (4)
- Fashionable young men (8)
- Fencing swords having a circular guard and thin, flexible blades (5)
- Feudal lord entitled to allegiance and service (5)
- Fishing with hook and line (7)
- Grass-like plants having solid stems, leaves in 3 vertical rows (6)
- Great destruction or devastation; ruinous damage (5)
- Humiliating or shameful; hurting one's pride or self-respect (10)
- Instruction by means of question and answer (11)
- Loud uproar, as from a crowd of people (6)
- Made filthy or dirty; unclean (7)
- Make clear or evident to the eye or the understanding (8)
- Misled by means of a petty trick or fraud; deceived (7)
- Noisy fight (4)
- Opposing and defeating the efforts, plans or ambitions of (9)
- Outward aspect or appearance (9)
- Painfully difficult or burdensome work; toil (7)
- Perforated utensil used for straining or sifting (5)
- Procedural directive or rule (10)
- Regarded or treated with haughty contempt; despised (9)
- Shaded or bordered with interlaced branches or vines (8)
- Showing contempt for (8)
- Simpleton; fool (3)
- Small drum (5)
- Speak of or treat slightly; depreciate; belittle (9)
- Stir, encourage, or urge on; stimulate or prompt to action (6)
- Sudden feeling of apprehensive uneasiness (5)
- Swashbuckler; one who delights in fighting (7)
- The art of writing (11)
- The quality of being devoutly religious (5)
- Type of stone showing curved, colored bands or other markings (5)
- Unit of distance equal to 3.0 statute miles (6)
- Unprincipled, untrustworthy, or dishonest person (5)
- Wall hanging, as a tapestry (5)
- Word or phrase applied to a person to describe an actual or attributed quality (7)

Much Ado Vocabulary Word Search 2 Answer Key

A fungal disease in plants or ulcer in animals; also, a variety of wildflower (6)
Agreeable; compatible (9)
Bestow or express excessive love or fondness habitually (4)
Boldness or determination in facing great danger (5)
Close-fitting outer garment worn by men in the Renaissance (7)
Cover for the crotch in men's hose or tight-fitting breeches (8)
Earthy mix of clay used as a fertilizer (4)
Fashionable young men (8)
Fencing swords having a circular guard and thin, flexible blades (5)
Feudal lord entitled to allegiance and service (5)
Fishing with hook and line (7)
Grass-like plants having solid stems, leaves in 3 vertical rows (6)
Great destruction or devastation; ruinous damage (5)
Humiliating or shameful; hurting one's pride or self-respect (10)
Instruction by means of question and answer (11)
Loud uproar, as from a crowd of people (6)
Made filthy or dirty; unclean (7)
Make clear or evident to the eye or the understanding (8)
Misled by means of a petty trick or fraud; deceived (7)

Noisy fight (4)
Opposing and defeating the efforts, plans or ambitions of (9)
Outward aspect or appearance (9)
Painfully difficult or burdensome work; toil (7)
Perforated utensil used for straining or sifting (5)
Procedural directive or rule (10)
Regarded or treated with haughty contempt; despised (9)
Shaded or bordered with interlaced branches or vines (8)
Showing contempt for (8)
Simpleton; fool (3)
Small drum (5)
Speak of or treat slightingly; depreciate; belittle (9)
Stir, encourage, or urge on; stimulate or prompt to action (6)
Sudden feeling of apprehensive uneasiness (5)
Swashbuckler; one who delights in fighting (7)
The art of writing (11)
The quality of being devoutly religious (5)
Type of stone showing curved, colored bands or other markings (5)
Unit of distance equal to 3.0 statute miles (6)
Unprincipled, untrustworthy, or dishonest person (5)
Wall hanging, as a tapestry (5)
Word or phrase applied to a person to describe an actual or attributed quality (7)

Much Ado Vocabulary Word Search 3

```
C I N Q U E P A C E A C C O R D A N T X
O O M I N O U S O L L S V P E R J U R Y
Z W V G I N F A M Y A I E P I E T Y W G
E K S E X T O N M Q L M E D X N C D Q Q
N I N C R E P R O V E S O G G D O I T R
E N D A C T Y M D F C H C R E E N S U H
D C O R V Q L V I T H R Y E Z R S P R C
V I U P X E S Y T C E E C Q G N T A N J
W T B I P B E Q Y A R W P U H D A R C Y
D E L N V I M C H N Y D V I D W B A O F
F O E G M N B B B K W F T T T G L G A M
M T T A R T L Y D E F I L E D H E E T S
M M G E R E A J Y R T O Y D D A E L M M
V M A Y Y R N B J M P R I Q H I W T E Q
C A L V F M C Z O A D O O L U I O D Z D
U N L F S I E V E R W Y N T S A T U J K
C I A O Y N J T K L T A G I H A L H S F
K F N F R G C A P O N R N G A S G M E C
O E T R J L E A G U E R D T V R N A N R
L S S A P E R T U R B A T I O N D P T X
D T X Y H A G G A R D S Y F C N C S K E
```

ACCORDANT	COZENED	HAGGARDS	OMINOUS	SHREWD
AGATE	CUCKOLD	HAVOC	PERJURY	SIEVE
ARRAS	CUDGELED	HITHER	PERTURBATION	TABOR
BETROTHS	DAW	INCITE	PIETY	TARTLY
CANKER	DEFILED	INFAMY	PONIARDS	TEDIOUS
CAPON	DISPARAGE	INTERMINGLE	QUALM	TURNCOAT
CARPING	DOTE	KNAVE	RENDER	VALOR
CINQUEPACE	DOUBLET	LEAGUE	REPROVE	WANTON
CLAMOR	EPITHET	LECHERY	REQUITED	
COMMODITY	FOILS	LIEGE	SEDGES	
CONSTABLE	FRAY	MANIFEST	SEMBLANCE	
COVERTLY	GALLANTS	MARL	SEXTON	

Much Ado Vocabulary Word Search 3 Answer Key

```
C I N Q U E P A C E A C C O R D A N T
O O M I N O U S O L L S   P E R J U R Y
Z V   I N F A M Y A I E P I E T Y
E K S E X T O N M   L M E D   N C D
N I N C R E P R O V E S O G G D O I T
E N D A   T     D   C H   R E E N S P   T U
D C O R V   L     I     H R     E     R S P   R N
    I U P   E S Y T C E E C Q       T A     N C
    T B I       E   Y A R W P U       A R     C O
D E L N     I M     N Y D   I D     B A     G O A
  O E G     N B     B K       T T G L G     A T
    T A R T L Y D E F I L E D H E E T
    G E     E A     R T O   D D A E L
V M A     R N B     M P R I Q H I W T   E
C A L     M C     O A   O O L U I O         D
U N L   S I E V E R W   N T S A T U
C I A O   N       L     A   I H A L H S
K F N F R G C A P O N R N   A S G M E
O E T R   L E A G U E R   T V R   A     R
L S S A P E R T U R B A T I O N D   T
D T   Y H A G G A R D S     C N   S     E
```

ACCORDANT   COZENED   HAGGARDS   OMINOUS   SHREWD

AGATE   CUCKOLD   HAVOC   PERJURY   SIEVE

ARRAS   CUDGELED   HITHER   PERTURBATION   TABOR

BETROTHS   DAW   INCITE   PIETY   TARTLY

CANKER   DEFILED   INFAMY   PONIARDS   TEDIOUS

CAPON   DISPARAGE   INTERMINGLE   QUALM   TURNCOAT

CARPING   DOTE   KNAVE   RENDER   VALOR

CINQUEPACE   DOUBLET   LEAGUE   REPROVE   WANTON

CLAMOR   EPITHET   LECHERY   REQUITED

COMMODITY   FOILS   LIEGE   SEDGES

CONSTABLE   FRAY   MANIFEST   SEMBLANCE

COVERTLY   GALLANTS   MARL   SEXTON

Much Ado Vocabulary Word Search 4

```
S E M B L A N C E C I N Q U E P A C E H
G E Y A E D C O Z E N E D R P L N T R V
A O X J R T A O B S T I N A T E D G B Q
L R R T M R W W B M E H A G G A R D S M
L V V T O A A I S C R U P L E C E Y F M
A I W R H N R S X G M D N W M H N T O S
N C L A M O R L M T I N P H A E D U I B
T T N V S K G D E W N I E N N D E R L M
S U H A H L V R L K G N R S I T R N S N
I A A I R D D C A N L F T E F A K C H Q
E L V L E G O O N P E A U D E B Y O I G
V W O V W H T X C P H M R G S O J A T N
E A C P D L E C H E R Y B E T R O T H S
Q N L A I O N O O R L O A S R A Q J E W
M F S O N E U M L F I M T W E A R L R X
B V K U R K T B Y U E I I B Q G G T P B
M I N C I T E Y L M G N O Q U A L M L C
F R A Y A N Q R N E E O N P I T B R B Y
M H V J K P G M B R T U R R T E P W H N
P L E D R F O L L I E S Y T E D I O U S
H E A R K E N N F W E X P E D I E N T V
```

AGATE	DOTE	HITHER	OMINOUS	SEMBLANCE
ARRAS	DOUBLET	INCITE	ORTHOGRAPHY	SEXTON
BETROTHS	ENSUING	INFAMY	PERFUMER	SHREWD
BETWIXT	EXPEDIENT	INTERMINGLE	PERTURBATION	SIEVE
CANKER	FOILS	KNAVE	PIETY	TABOR
CAPON	FOLLIES	LECHERY	PLEACHED	TARTLY
CINQUEPACE	FRAY	LIEGE	QUALM	TEDIOUS
CLAMOR	GALLANTS	MANIFEST	RENDER	TRAVAIL
COXCOMB	HAGGARDS	MARL	REQUITED	TURNCOAT
COZENED	HAVOC	MELANCHOLY	SCRUPLE	VALOR
DAW	HEARKEN	OBSTINATE	SEDGES	VICTUAL

Much Ado Vocabulary Word Search 4 Answer Key

AGATE	DOTE	HITHER	OMINOUS	SEMBLANCE
ARRAS	DOUBLET	INCITE	ORTHOGRAPHY	SEXTON
BETROTHS	ENSUING	INFAMY	PERFUMER	SHREWD
BETWIXT	EXPEDIENT	INTERMINGLE	PERTURBATION	SIEVE
CANKER	FOILS	KNAVE	PIETY	TABOR
CAPON	FOLLIES	LECHERY	PLEACHED	TARTLY
CINQUEPACE	FRAY	LIEGE	QUALM	TEDIOUS
CLAMOR	GALLANTS	MANIFEST	RENDER	TRAVAIL
COXCOMB	HAGGARDS	MARL	REQUITED	TURNCOAT
COZENED	HAVOC	MELANCHOLY	SCRUPLE	VALOR
DAW	HEARKEN	OBSTINATE	SEDGES	VICTUAL

Much Ado Vocabulary Crossword 1

Across
1. Word or phrase applied to a person to describe an actual or attributed quality
4. Wall hanging, as a tapestry
6. Swashbuckler; one who delights in fighting
7. In a concealed, secret, or disguised manner
10. Simpleton; fool
11. Lively dance, the steps of which were regulated by the number 5
12. Noisy fight
15. Earthy mix of clay used as a fertilizer
19. Deadly or virulent epidemic disease
21. Type of stone showing curved, colored bands or other markings
22. Bestow or express excessive love or fondness habitually
23. Sharp or ill-tempered

Down
1. Following as a consequence or result
2. Painfully difficult or burdensome work; toil
3. Person who changes to an opposing idea or reverses principles
5. Very small portion or amount
7. A fungal disease in plants or ulcer in animals; also, a variety of wildflower
8. Allow or permit, as by favor or graciousness
9. Unrestrained or excessive indulgence of sexual desire
13. Castrated male chicken
14. Portending evil or harm; foreboding; threatening
16. Feudal lord entitled to allegiance and service
17. Provide; submit for inspection
18. The quality of being devoutly religious
20. Perforated utensil used for straining or sifting

Much Ado Vocabulary Crossword 1 Answer Key

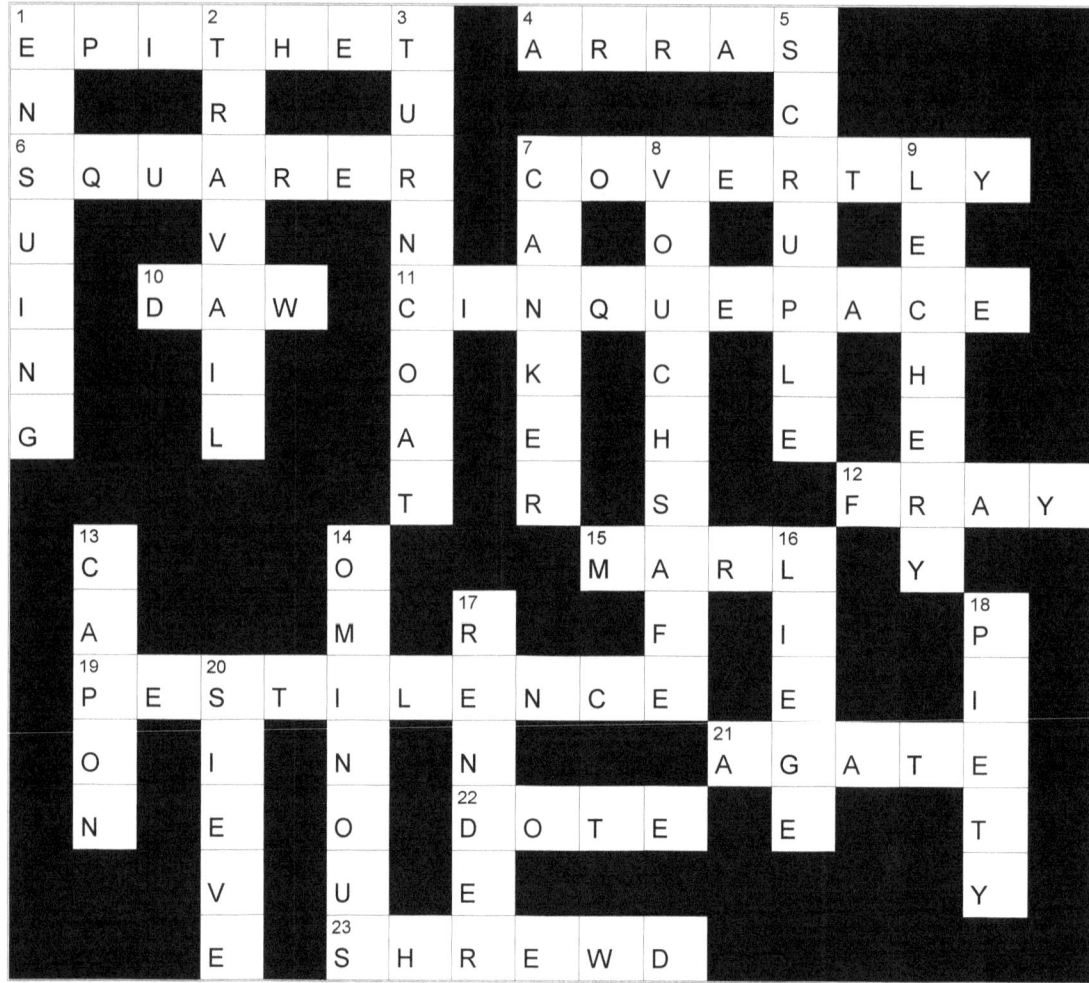

Across
1. Word or phrase applied to a person to describe an actual or attributed quality
4. Wall hanging, as a tapestry
6. Swashbuckler; one who delights in fighting
7. In a concealed, secret, or disguised manner
10. Simpleton; fool
11. Lively dance, the steps of which were regulated by the number 5
12. Noisy fight
15. Earthy mix of clay used as a fertilizer
19. Deadly or virulent epidemic disease
21. Type of stone showing curved, colored bands or other markings
22. Bestow or express excessive love or fondness habitually
23. Sharp or ill-tempered

Down
1. Following as a consequence or result
2. Painfully difficult or burdensome work; toil
3. Person who changes to an opposing idea or reverses principles
5. Very small portion or amount
7. A fungal disease in plants or ulcer in animals; also, a variety of wildflower
8. Allow or permit, as by favor or graciousness
9. Unrestrained or excessive indulgence of sexual desire
13. Castrated male chicken
14. Portending evil or harm; foreboding; threatening
16. Feudal lord entitled to allegiance and service
17. Provide; submit for inspection
18. The quality of being devoutly religious
20. Perforated utensil used for straining or sifting

Much Ado Vocabulary Crossword 2

Across
2. Acts lacking good sense, understanding, or foresight
6. Shaded or bordered with interlaced branches or vines
9. Type of stone showing curved, colored bands or other markings
10. Person employed to take care of a church
11. One who makes or sells perfumes
14. Fencing swords having a circular guard and thin, flexible blades
17. Swashbuckler; one who delights in fighting
19. Word or phrase applied to a person to describe an actual or attributed quality
20. Between; in the middle
22. Unprincipled, untrustworthy, or dishonest person
23. Rascal; a knave

Down
1. Belong as a part, right, possession, or attribute
2. Noisy fight
3. Feudal lord entitled to allegiance and service
4. Extremely bad reputation
5. Very small portion or amount
7. A fungal disease in plants or ulcer in animals; also, a variety of wildflower
8. Simpleton; fool
12. Following as a consequence or result
13. Earthy mix of clay used as a fertilizer
15. Portending evil or harm; foreboding; threatening
16. Perforated utensil used for straining or sifting
18. Provide; submit for inspection
21. Small drum

Much Ado Vocabulary Crossword 2 Answer Key

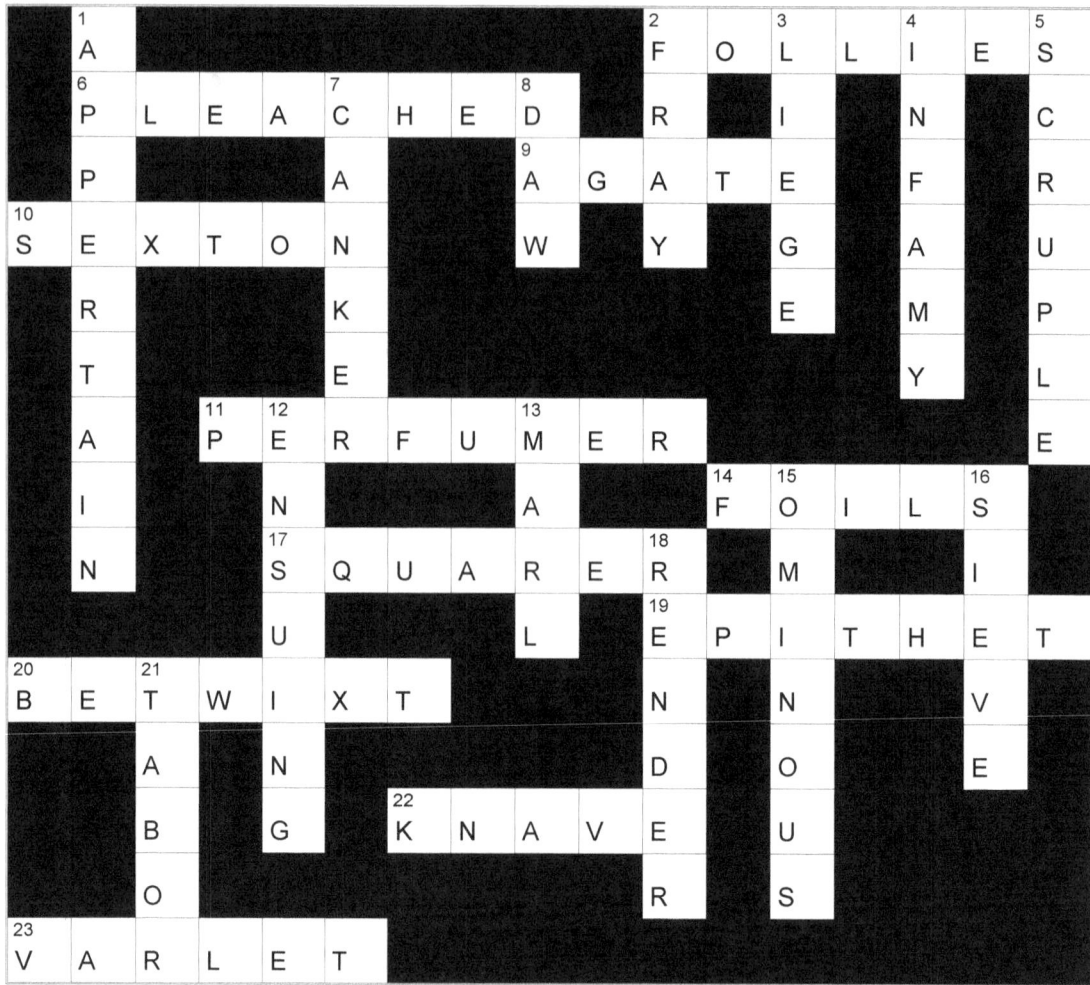

Across
2. Acts lacking good sense, understanding, or foresight
6. Shaded or bordered with interlaced branches or vines
9. Type of stone showing curved, colored bands or other markings
10. Person employed to take care of a church
11. One who makes or sells perfumes
14. Fencing swords having a circular guard and thin, flexible blades
17. Swashbuckler; one who delights in fighting
19. Word or phrase applied to a person to describe an actual or attributed quality
20. Between; in the middle
22. Unprincipled, untrustworthy, or dishonest person
23. Rascal; a knave

Down
1. Belong as a part, right, possession, or attribute
2. Noisy fight
3. Feudal lord entitled to allegiance and service
4. Extremely bad reputation
5. Very small portion or amount
7. A fungal disease in plants or ulcer in animals; also, a variety of wildflower
8. Simpleton; fool
12. Following as a consequence or result
13. Earthy mix of clay used as a fertilizer
15. Portending evil or harm; foreboding; threatening
16. Perforated utensil used for straining or sifting
18. Provide; submit for inspection
21. Small drum

Much Ado Vocabulary Crossword 3

Across
1. Rascal; a knave
4. A fungal disease in plants or ulcer in animals; also, a variety of wildflower
8. Between; in the middle
10. Simpleton; fool
11. Give heed or attention to what is said; listen
12. Earthy mix of clay used as a fertilizer
13. Close-fitting outer garment worn by men in the Renaissance
16. Perforated utensil used for straining or sifting
19. Swashbuckler; one who delights in fighting
20. Misled by means of a petty trick or fraud; deceived
21. Showing contempt for
22. Bestow or express excessive love or fondness habitually

Down
2. Type of stone showing curved, colored bands or other markings
3. Those who act without moral restraint
4. Vain and often foolish person
5. Unprincipled, untrustworthy, or dishonest person
6. Being saved from error or evil
7. Opposing and defeating the efforts, plans or ambitions of
9. Sexually lawless or unrestrained
11. Adult hawks captured for training
14. Feudal lord entitled to allegiance and service
15. Person who changes to an opposing idea or reverses principles
17. Grass-like plants having solid stems, leaves in 3 vertical rows
18. Sudden feeling of apprehensive uneasiness

Much Ado Vocabulary Crossword 3 Answer Key

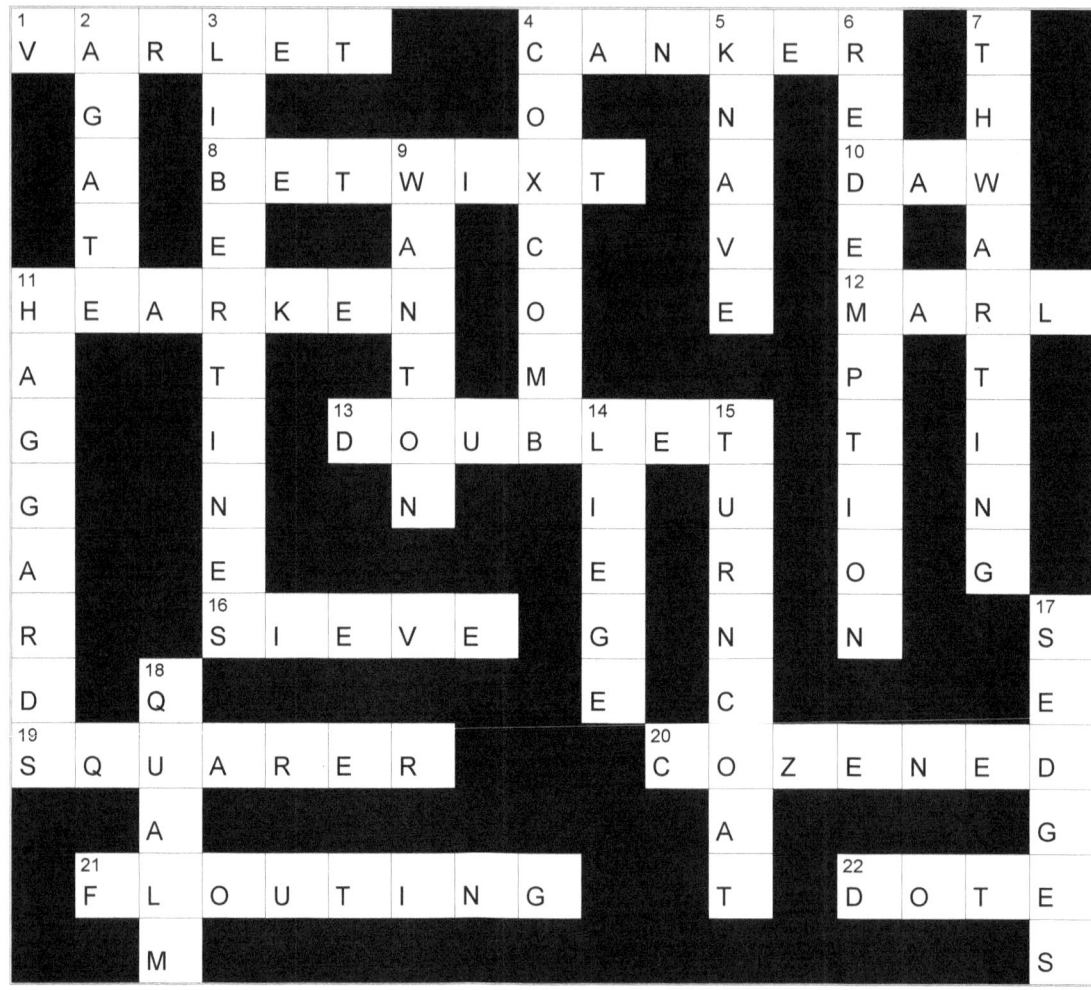

Across
1. Rascal; a knave
4. A fungal disease in plants or ulcer in animals; also, a variety of wildflower
8. Between; in the middle
10. Simpleton; fool
11. Give heed or attention to what is said; listen
12. Earthy mix of clay used as a fertilizer
13. Close-fitting outer garment worn by men in the Renaissance
16. Perforated utensil used for straining or sifting
19. Swashbuckler; one who delights in fighting
20. Misled by means of a petty trick or fraud; deceived
21. Showing contempt for
22. Bestow or express excessive love or fondness habitually

Down
2. Type of stone showing curved, colored bands or other markings
3. Those who act without moral restraint
4. Vain and often foolish person
5. Unprincipled, untrustworthy, or dishonest person
6. Being saved from error or evil
7. Opposing and defeating the efforts, plans or ambitions of
9. Sexually lawless or unrestrained
11. Adult hawks captured for training
14. Feudal lord entitled to allegiance and service
15. Person who changes to an opposing idea or reverses principles
17. Grass-like plants having solid stems, leaves in 3 vertical rows
18. Sudden feeling of apprehensive uneasiness

Much Ado Vocabulary Crossword 4

Across
1. Between; in the middle
5. Type of stone showing curved, colored bands or other markings
7. Humiliating or shameful; hurting one's pride or self-respect
8. Being saved from error or evil
15. Painfully difficult or burdensome work; toil
17. Sudden feeling of apprehensive uneasiness
18. Small drum
20. Castrated male chicken
21. Grass-like plants having solid stems, leaves in 3 vertical rows
22. Shaded or bordered with interlaced branches or vines
23. Bestow or express excessive love or fondness habitually

Down
2. Sexually lawless or unrestrained
3. Sharply; in a cutting manner
4. One who makes or sells perfumes
6. Agreeable; compatible
7. Earthy mix of clay used as a fertilizer
9. Perplexing; mysterious
10. The quality of being devoutly religious
11. Noisy fight
12. Simpleton; fool
13. Rascal; a knave
14. Swashbuckler; one who delights in fighting
16. Unit of distance equal to 3.0 statute miles
19. Feudal lord entitled to allegiance and service

Much Ado Vocabulary Crossword 4 Answer Key

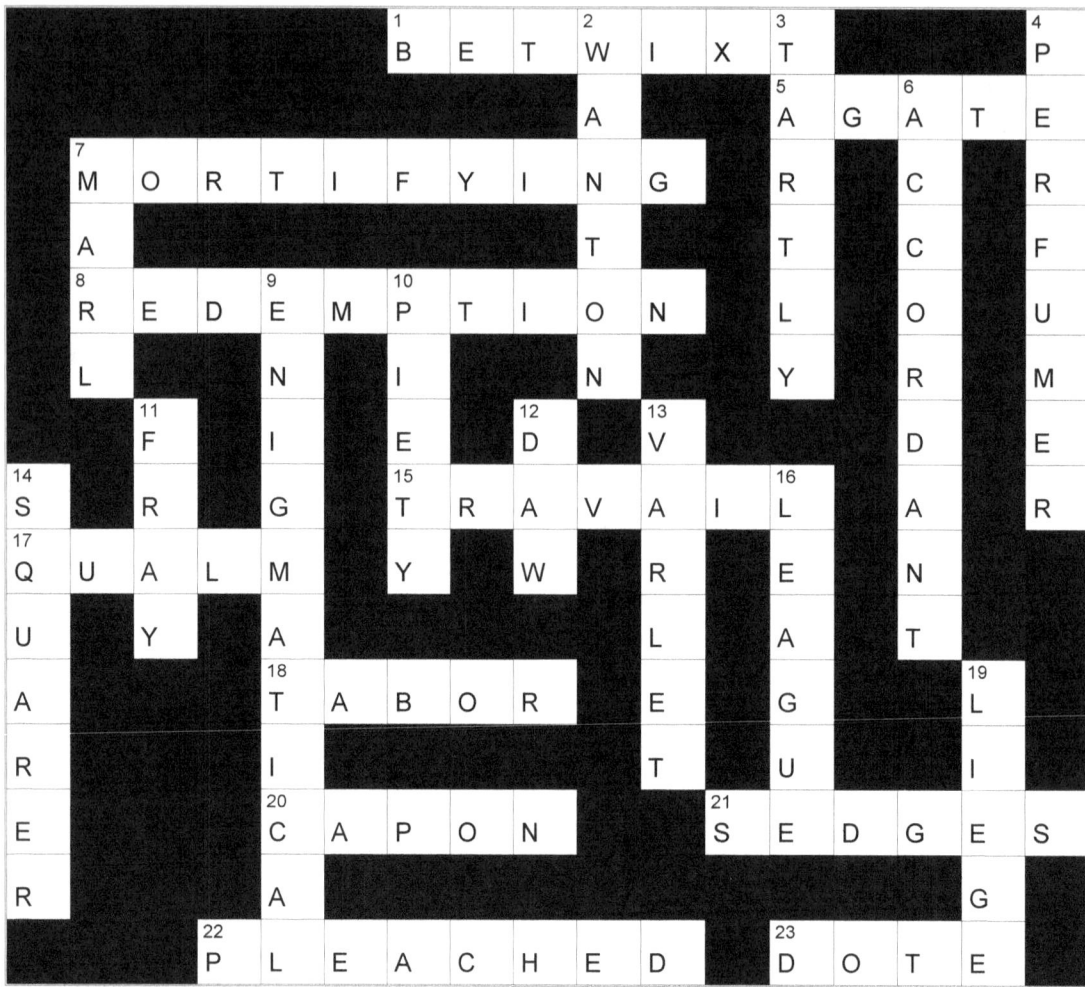

Across
1. Between; in the middle
5. Type of stone showing curved, colored bands or other markings
7. Humiliating or shameful; hurting one's pride or self-respect
8. Being saved from error or evil
15. Painfully difficult or burdensome work; toil
17. Sudden feeling of apprehensive uneasiness
18. Small drum
20. Castrated male chicken
21. Grass-like plants having solid stems, leaves in 3 vertical rows
22. Shaded or bordered with interlaced branches or vines
23. Bestow or express excessive love or fondness habitually

Down
2. Sexually lawless or unrestrained
3. Sharply; in a cutting manner
4. One who makes or sells perfumes
6. Agreeable; compatible
7. Earthy mix of clay used as a fertilizer
9. Perplexing; mysterious
10. The quality of being devoutly religious
11. Noisy fight
12. Simpleton; fool
13. Rascal; a knave
14. Swashbuckler; one who delights in fighting
16. Unit of distance equal to 3.0 statute miles
19. Feudal lord entitled to allegiance and service

Much Ado Vocabulary Juggle Letters 1

1. NQPEIUACEC = 1. _____
   Lively dance, the steps of which were regulated by the number 5

2. SPGAEDARI = 2. _____
   Speak of or treat slightingly; depreciate; belittle

3. ELTYCRVO = 3. _____
   In a concealed, secret, or disguised manner

4. KENCGIRON = 4. _____
   Settlement of accounts or of a score

5. VEISE = 5. _____
   Perforated utensil used for straining or sifting

6. NODSAPIR = 6. _____
   Daggers typically having slender square or triangular blades

7. EDDFILE = 7. _____
   Made filthy or dirty; unclean

8. MLRA = 8. _____
   Earthy mix of clay used as a fertilizer

9. LUBTEOD = 9. _____
   Close-fitting outer garment worn by men in the Renaissance

10. EIGRMLNTENI =10. _____
    Mix or become mixed together

11. TTNIEATSOON =11. _____
    Conspicuous show or display intended to impress others

12. TOMIMDOYC =12. _____
    Article of trade or commerce

13. EEDIQRUT =13. _____
    Made a payment or return for

14. ERAQUSR =14. _____
    Swashbuckler; one who delights in fighting

Much Ado Vocabulary Juggle Letters 1 Answer Key

1. NQPEIUACEC = 1. CINQUEPACE
   Lively dance, the steps of which were regulated by the number 5

2. SPGAEDARI = 2. DISPARAGE
   Speak of or treat slightingly; depreciate; belittle

3. ELTYCRVO = 3. COVERTLY
   In a concealed, secret, or disguised manner

4. KENCGIRON = 4. RECKONING
   Settlement of accounts or of a score

5. VEISE = 5. SIEVE
   Perforated utensil used for straining or sifting

6. NODSAPIR = 6. PONIARDS
   Daggers typically having slender square or triangular blades

7. EDDFILE = 7. DEFILED
   Made filthy or dirty; unclean

8. MLRA = 8. MARL
   Earthy mix of clay used as a fertilizer

9. LUBTEOD = 9. DOUBLET
   Close-fitting outer garment worn by men in the Renaissance

10. EIGRMLNTENI = 10. INTERMINGLE
    Mix or become mixed together

11. TTNIEATSOON = 11. OSTENTATION
    Conspicuous show or display intended to impress others

12. TOMIMDOYC = 12. COMMODITY
    Article of trade or commerce

13. EEDIQRUT = 13. REQUITED
    Made a payment or return for

14. ERAQUSR = 14. SQUARER
    Swashbuckler; one who delights in fighting

Much Ado Vocabulary Juggle Letters 2

1. ZGENIITCHCA = 1. _____
   Instruction by means of question and answer

2. TIUALCV = 2. _____
   Food supply; provisions

3. AQUML = 3. _____
   Sudden feeling of apprehensive uneasiness

4. SDGEES = 4. _____
   Grass-like plants having solid stems, leaves in 3 vertical rows

5. EEDDIFL = 5. _____
   Made filthy or dirty; unclean

6. VIEES = 6. _____
   Perforated utensil used for straining or sifting

7. IFYRNGTIMO = 7. _____
   Humiliating or shameful; hurting one's pride or self-respect

8. AMLR = 8. _____
   Earthy mix of clay used as a fertilizer

9. CPNSITEELE = 9. _____
   Deadly or virulent epidemic disease

10. REMRUEPF = 10. _____
    One who makes or sells perfumes

11. DDNDIIASE = 11. _____
    Regarded or treated with haughty contempt; despised

12. RBTOA = 12. _____
    Small drum

13. CNROCADAT = 13. _____
    Agreeable; compatible

14. LSNGATAL = 14. _____
    Fashionable young men

Much Ado Vocabulary Juggle Letters 2 Answer Key

1. ZGENIITCHCA = 1. CATECHIZING
Instruction by means of question and answer

2. TIUALCV = 2. VICTUAL
Food supply; provisions

3. AQUML = 3. QUALM
Sudden feeling of apprehensive uneasiness

4. SDGEES = 4. SEDGES
Grass-like plants having solid stems, leaves in 3 vertical rows

5. EEDDIFL = 5. DEFILED
Made filthy or dirty; unclean

6. VIEES = 6. SIEVE
Perforated utensil used for straining or sifting

7. IFYRNGTIMO = 7. MORTIFYING
Humiliating or shameful; hurting one's pride or self-respect

8. AMLR = 8. MARL
Earthy mix of clay used as a fertilizer

9. CPNSITEELE = 9. PESTILENCE
Deadly or virulent epidemic disease

10. REMRUEPF = 10. PERFUMER
One who makes or sells perfumes

11. DDNDIIASE = 11. DISDAINED
Regarded or treated with haughty contempt; despised

12. RBTOA = 12. TABOR
Small drum

13. CNROCADAT = 13. ACCORDANT
Agreeable; compatible

14. LSNGATAL = 14. GALLANTS
Fashionable young men

Much Ado Vocabulary Juggle Letters 3

1. GAATE = 1. _____
Type of stone showing curved, colored bands or other markings

2. TURAVDEPENRE = 2. _____
By chance; with doubt or uncertainty

3. NPITAEPAR = 3. _____
Belong as a part, right, possession, or attribute

4. ECEPODIC = 4. _____
Cover for the crotch in men's hose or tight-fitting breeches

5. ECLDEAHP = 5. _____
Shaded or bordered with interlaced branches or vines

6. RYPRUEJ = 6. _____
Willful giving of false testimony under oath

7. ALATNSGL = 7. _____
Fashionable young men

8. VCAOH = 8. _____
Great destruction or devastation; ruinous damage

9. UCOTRANT = 9. _____
Person who changes to an opposing idea or reverses principles

10. HOAHYTRPRGO = 10. _____
The art of writing

11. ELBDOUT = 11. _____
Close-fitting outer garment worn by men in the Renaissance

12. SPELCTEIEN = 12. _____
Deadly or virulent epidemic disease

13. EOFLLSI = 13. _____
Acts lacking good sense, understanding, or foresight

14. OCUCKDL = 14. _____
Husband of an unfaithful wife

Much Ado Vocabulary Juggle Letters 3 Answer Key

1. GAATE = 1. AGATE
   Type of stone showing curved, colored bands or other markings

2. TURAVDEPENRE = 2. PERADVENTURE
   By chance; with doubt or uncertainty

3. NPITAEPAR = 3. APPERTAIN
   Belong as a part, right, possession, or attribute

4. ECEPODIC = 4. CODPIECE
   Cover for the crotch in men's hose or tight-fitting breeches

5. ECLDEAHP = 5. PLEACHED
   Shaded or bordered with interlaced branches or vines

6. RYPRUEJ = 6. PERJURY
   Willful giving of false testimony under oath

7. ALATNSGL = 7. GALLANTS
   Fashionable young men

8. VCAOH = 8. HAVOC
   Great destruction or devastation; ruinous damage

9. UCOTRANT = 9. TURNCOAT
   Person who changes to an opposing idea or reverses principles

10. HOAHYTRPRGO = 10. ORTHOGRAPHY
    The art of writing

11. ELBDOUT = 11. DOUBLET
    Close-fitting outer garment worn by men in the Renaissance

12. SPELCTEIEN = 12. PESTILENCE
    Deadly or virulent epidemic disease

13. EOFLLSI = 13. FOLLIES
    Acts lacking good sense, understanding, or foresight

14. OCUCKDL = 14. CUCKOLD
    Husband of an unfaithful wife

Much Ado Vocabulary Juggle Letters 4

1. TABEOSCNL = 1. _____
   Officer of the peace having police and minor judicial functions

2. OEDTUBL = 2. _____
   Close-fitting outer garment worn by men in the Renaissance

3. LSLEIOF = 3. _____
   Acts lacking good sense, understanding, or foresight

4. ODULCKC = 4. _____
   Husband of an unfaithful wife

5. KNGCORNIE = 5. _____
   Settlement of accounts or of a score

6. EERAHKN = 6. _____
   Give heed or attention to what is said; listen

7. TXWBTIE = 7. _____
   Between; in the middle

8. ATCTORUN = 8. _____
   Person who changes to an opposing idea or reverses principles

9. LAITRAV = 9. _____
   Painfully difficult or burdensome work; toil

10. TYMDCIOOM =10. _____
    Article of trade or commerce

11. EEVIS =11. _____
    Perforated utensil used for straining or sifting

12. DESSGE =12. _____
    Grass-like plants having solid stems, leaves in 3 vertical rows

13. CSPNEEITEL =13. _____
    Deadly or virulent epidemic disease

14. CELYREH =14. _____
    Unrestrained or excessive indulgence of sexual desire

Much Ado Vocabulary Juggle Letters 4 Answer Key

1. TABEOSCNL = 1. CONSTABLE
Officer of the peace having police and minor judicial functions

2. OEDTUBL = 2. DOUBLET
Close-fitting outer garment worn by men in the Renaissance

3. LSLEIOF = 3. FOLLIES
Acts lacking good sense, understanding, or foresight

4. ODULCKC = 4. CUCKOLD
Husband of an unfaithful wife

5. KNGCORNIE = 5. RECKONING
Settlement of accounts or of a score

6. EERAHKN = 6. HEARKEN
Give heed or attention to what is said; listen

7. TXWBTIE = 7. BETWIXT
Between; in the middle

8. ATCTORUN = 8. TURNCOAT
Person who changes to an opposing idea or reverses principles

9. LAITRAV = 9. TRAVAIL
Painfully difficult or burdensome work; toil

10. TYMDCIOOM = 10. COMMODITY
Article of trade or commerce

11. EEVIS = 11. SIEVE
Perforated utensil used for straining or sifting

12. DESSGE = 12. SEDGES
Grass-like plants having solid stems, leaves in 3 vertical rows

13. CSPNEEITEL = 13. PESTILENCE
Deadly or virulent epidemic disease

14. CELYREH = 14. LECHERY
Unrestrained or excessive indulgence of sexual desire

ACCORDANT	Agreeable; compatible
AGATE	Type of stone showing curved, colored bands or other markings
ANGLING	Fishing with hook and line
APPERTAIN	Belong as a part, right, possession, or attribute
ARRAS	Wall hanging, as a tapestry

BETROTHS	Promises to give in marriage
BETWIXT	Between; in the middle
CANKER	A fungal disease in plants or ulcer in animals; also, a variety of wildflower
CAPON	Castrated male chicken
CARPING	Petty fault-finding

CATECHIZING	Instruction by means of question and answer
CINQUEPACE	Lively dance, the steps of which were regulated by the number 5
CLAMOR	Loud uproar, as from a crowd of people
CODPIECE	Cover for the crotch in men's hose or tight-fitting breeches
COMMODITY	Article of trade or commerce

CONSTABLE	Officer of the peace having police and minor judicial functions
COVERTLY	In a concealed, secret, or disguised manner
COXCOMB	Vain and often foolish person
COZENED	Misled by means of a petty trick or fraud; deceived
CUCKOLD	Husband of an unfaithful wife

CUDGELED	Struck or beat with a stick
DAW	Simpleton; fool
DEFILED	Made filthy or dirty; unclean
DISDAINED	Regarded or treated with haughty contempt; despised
DISPARAGE	Speak of or treat slightly; depreciate; belittle

DISSEMBLER	One who gives a false or misleading appearance
DISSUADE	Advise or urge against
DOTE	Bestow or express excessive love or fondness habitually
DOUBLET	Close-fitting outer garment worn by men in the Renaissance
ENFRANCHISED	Freed, as from bondage

ENIGMATICAL	Perplexing; mysterious
ENSUING	Following as a consequence or result
EPITHET	Word or phrase applied to a person to describe an actual or attributed quality
EXPEDIENT	Fit or suitable for the purpose; proper under the circumstances
FLOUTING	Showing contempt for

FOILS	Fencing swords having a circular guard and thin, flexible blades
FOLLIES	Acts lacking good sense, understanding, or foresight
FRAY	Noisy fight
GALLANTS	Fashionable young men
HAGGARDS	Adult hawks captured for training

HAVOC	Great destruction or devastation; ruinous damage
HEARKEN	Give heed or attention to what is said; listen
HITHER	To or toward this place
IMPEDIMENT	Obstruction; hindrance; obstacle
INCITE	Stir, encourage, or urge on; stimulate or prompt to action

INFAMY	Extremely bad reputation
INTERMINGLE	Mix or become mixed together
KNAVE	Unprincipled, untrustworthy, or dishonest person
LEAGUE	Unit of distance equal to 3.0 statute miles
LECHERY	Unrestrained or excessive indulgence of sexual desire

LIBERTINES	Those who act without moral restraint
LIEGE	Feudal lord entitled to allegiance and service
MALEFACTORS	Those who have committed a crime; criminals
MANIFEST	Make clear or evident to the eye or the understanding
MARL	Earthy mix of clay used as a fertilizer

MELANCHOLY	Gloomy state of mind; depression
MORTIFYING	Humiliating or shameful; hurting one's pride or self-respect
OBSTINATE	Firmly or stubbornly holding to one's purpose or opinion
OMINOUS	Portending evil or harm; foreboding; threatening
ORTHOGRAPHY	The art of writing

OSTENTATION	Conspicuous show or display intended to impress others
PERADVENTURE	By chance; with doubt or uncertainty
PERFUMER	One who makes or sells perfumes
PERJURY	Willful giving of false testimony under oath
PERNICIOUS	Causing harm or ruin

PERTURBATION	Mental disquiet, disturbance, or agitation
PESTILENCE	Deadly or virulent epidemic disease
PIETY	The quality of being devoutly religious
PLEACHED	Shaded or bordered with interlaced branches or vines
PONIARDS	Daggers typically having slender square or triangular blades

PRECEPTIAL	Procedural directive or rule
QUALM	Sudden feeling of apprehensive uneasiness
RECKONING	Settlement of accounts or of a score
REDEMPTION	Being saved from error or evil
RENDER	Provide; submit for inspection

REPROVE	Criticize or correct
REQUITED	Made a payment or return for
SCRUPLE	Very small portion or amount
SEDGES	Grass-like plants having solid stems, leaves in 3 vertical rows
SEMBLANCE	Outward aspect or appearance

SEXTON	Person employed to take care of a church
SHREWD	Sharp or ill-tempered
SIEVE	Perforated utensil used for straining or sifting
SLANDERED	Made false and malicious statements or reports about someone
SQUARER	Swashbuckler; one who delights in fighting

TABOR	Small drum
TARTLY	Sharply; in a cutting manner
TEDIOUS	Boring, tiring, monotonous, dull
THWARTING	Opposing and defeating the efforts, plans or ambitions of
TRAVAIL	Painfully difficult or burdensome work; toil

TURNCOAT	Person who changes to an opposing idea or reverses principles
VALOR	Boldness or determination in facing great danger
VARLET	Rascal; a knave
VICTUAL	Food supply; provisions
VOUCHSAFE	Allow or permit, as by favor or graciousness

WANTON

Sexually lawless or unrestrained

Much Ado Vocabulary

MANIFEST	DISSEMBLER	TURNCOAT	CATECHIZING	PONIARDS
THWARTING	HAVOC	SEDGES	OSTENTATION	QUALM
ACCORDANT	CUCKOLD	FREE SPACE	MORTIFYING	ANGLING
SLANDERED	ENIGMATICAL	CANKER	SHREWD	ENFRANCHISED
REDEMPTION	FOILS	PESTILENCE	SIEVE	COMMODITY

Much Ado Vocabulary

COZENED	PERJURY	DISPARAGE	INTERMINGLE	RENDER
DISDAINED	TARTLY	MARL	PERFUMER	OBSTINATE
CLAMOR	RECKONING	FREE SPACE	DEFILED	SEXTON
COVERTLY	LIBERTINES	REQUITED	SCRUPLE	CINQUEPACE
DOUBLET	SQUARER	APPERTAIN	CUDGELED	EXPEDIENT

Much Ado Vocabulary

KNAVE	CUDGELED	HAVOC	ENIGMATICAL	IMPEDIMENT
CONSTABLE	RECKONING	VALOR	CLAMOR	CATECHIZING
ENSUING	MORTIFYING	FREE SPACE	ANGLING	HEARKEN
DISSEMBLER	LIBERTINES	OSTENTATION	SQUARER	FOILS
SIEVE	TRAVAIL	COXCOMB	FLOUTING	TABOR

Much Ado Vocabulary

DISDAINED	PERADVENTURE	PERTURBATION	PERNICIOUS	PESTILENCE
DISPARAGE	FRAY	CINQUEPACE	CAPON	MELANCHOLY
SEMBLANCE	COVERTLY	FREE SPACE	HAGGARDS	SEXTON
FOLLIES	TEDIOUS	LEAGUE	EPITHET	VOUCHSAFE
LIEGE	CUCKOLD	CARPING	DISSUADE	DOUBLET

Much Ado Vocabulary

DEFILED	ACCORDANT	AGATE	CODPIECE	PIETY
HITHER	ANGLING	PONIARDS	SQUARER	CARPING
CANKER	MARL	FREE SPACE	COMMODITY	LECHERY
SHREWD	DISPARAGE	RENDER	INCITE	REQUITED
SEDGES	VOUCHSAFE	PERADVENTURE	TABOR	CAPON

Much Ado Vocabulary

LEAGUE	ENIGMATICAL	PERTURBATION	CUCKOLD	OMINOUS
DISSEMBLER	OBSTINATE	HEARKEN	SEXTON	TEDIOUS
COVERTLY	INTERMINGLE	FREE SPACE	APPERTAIN	TARTLY
FRAY	DOTE	PERJURY	HAVOC	PERFUMER
THWARTING	DOUBLET	FLOUTING	VICTUAL	SEMBLANCE

Much Ado Vocabulary

ANGLING	OBSTINATE	ENFRANCHISED	APPERTAIN	INFAMY
CATECHIZING	KNAVE	FOILS	LIEGE	SQUARER
PERJURY	ORTHOGRAPHY	FREE SPACE	PLEACHED	IMPEDIMENT
ACCORDANT	REQUITED	HAVOC	FLOUTING	PESTILENCE
MELANCHOLY	DOUBLET	BETWIXT	PERADVENTURE	DEFILED

Much Ado Vocabulary

OMINOUS	VICTUAL	PERFUMER	BETROTHS	THWARTING
AGATE	CLAMOR	DISPARAGE	DOTE	DISDAINED
CONSTABLE	CUCKOLD	FREE SPACE	CODPIECE	QUALM
WANTON	TABOR	RENDER	CUDGELED	DISSUADE
SEXTON	LEAGUE	PIETY	TARTLY	SEMBLANCE

Much Ado Vocabulary

CONSTABLE	OSTENTATION	REDEMPTION	TABOR	VICTUAL
SEXTON	RENDER	PERADVENTURE	SIEVE	PERFUMER
LECHERY	CINQUEPACE	FREE SPACE	TRAVAIL	COMMODITY
LIBERTINES	KNAVE	CANKER	CLAMOR	EPITHET
SQUARER	COXCOMB	PERNICIOUS	GALLANTS	DISSUADE

Much Ado Vocabulary

MELANCHOLY	ACCORDANT	CAPON	DOTE	FLOUTING
SHREWD	ANGLING	ENFRANCHISED	DEFILED	DISSEMBLER
QUALM	SCRUPLE	FREE SPACE	PRECEPTIAL	WANTON
INFAMY	TARTLY	LIEGE	PESTILENCE	FOLLIES
MARL	INTERMINGLE	REQUITED	FOILS	HITHER

Much Ado Vocabulary

HEARKEN	ACCORDANT	PERTURBATION	APPERTAIN	RENDER
SEXTON	COXCOMB	FOLLIES	REPROVE	ORTHOGRAPHY
DISPARAGE	PLEACHED	FREE SPACE	TABOR	OMINOUS
SLANDERED	LECHERY	REDEMPTION	TURNCOAT	CUCKOLD
MARL	GALLANTS	HAGGARDS	SEDGES	SHREWD

Much Ado Vocabulary

DISDAINED	TEDIOUS	QUALM	TRAVAIL	RECKONING
WANTON	OSTENTATION	COVERTLY	VARLET	PRECEPTIAL
MELANCHOLY	CATECHIZING	FREE SPACE	CLAMOR	IMPEDIMENT
DOTE	LEAGUE	VICTUAL	SCRUPLE	THWARTING
INFAMY	INCITE	CONSTABLE	ARRAS	SEMBLANCE

Much Ado Vocabulary

INTERMINGLE	SHREWD	SEDGES	PERFUMER	PONIARDS
TEDIOUS	DISPARAGE	TURNCOAT	MALEFACTORS	RECKONING
APPERTAIN	ENFRANCHISED	FREE SPACE	DISDAINED	FOILS
DAW	CANKER	CODPIECE	SEXTON	MORTIFYING
HAGGARDS	DISSEMBLER	DEFILED	SIEVE	CLAMOR

Much Ado Vocabulary

DISSUADE	COXCOMB	TABOR	MANIFEST	EPITHET
RENDER	ARRAS	PLEACHED	ENSUING	TRAVAIL
PRECEPTIAL	INFAMY	FREE SPACE	OBSTINATE	IMPEDIMENT
CINQUEPACE	FOLLIES	HEARKEN	EXPEDIENT	LIEGE
MELANCHOLY	CONSTABLE	HITHER	WANTON	PIETY

Much Ado Vocabulary

CATECHIZING	DEFILED	EPITHET	PERNICIOUS	LIEGE
HAVOC	COMMODITY	SEDGES	VALOR	SEXTON
INCITE	CONSTABLE	FREE SPACE	LIBERTINES	ENIGMATICAL
QUALM	CINQUEPACE	SCRUPLE	OSTENTATION	PESTILENCE
IMPEDIMENT	RENDER	GALLANTS	LECHERY	PERTURBATION

Much Ado Vocabulary

PERADVENTURE	TRAVAIL	CODPIECE	REPROVE	REQUITED
MANIFEST	PONIARDS	CUCKOLD	CARPING	SHREWD
WANTON	PERJURY	FREE SPACE	SIEVE	TEDIOUS
MARL	DAW	FOLLIES	MORTIFYING	TABOR
MALEFACTORS	TARTLY	RECKONING	THWARTING	ANGLING

Much Ado Vocabulary

ENFRANCHISED	PERFUMER	FOILS	SCRUPLE	COVERTLY
PONIARDS	CLAMOR	TEDIOUS	IMPEDIMENT	REDEMPTION
SLANDERED	DISPARAGE	FREE SPACE	REPROVE	TABOR
FOLLIES	GALLANTS	CANKER	COXCOMB	BETWIXT
TRAVAIL	DAW	PERADVENTURE	ACCORDANT	MANIFEST

Much Ado Vocabulary

CUCKOLD	PRECEPTIAL	INTERMINGLE	ENIGMATICAL	INCITE
ENSUING	PERNICIOUS	CUDGELED	CONSTABLE	KNAVE
RENDER	ARRAS	FREE SPACE	DISSEMBLER	EPITHET
HAVOC	MORTIFYING	SEXTON	OBSTINATE	APPERTAIN
SEDGES	INFAMY	PERJURY	LEAGUE	COZENED

Much Ado Vocabulary

SQUARER	DISPARAGE	PESTILENCE	DISSUADE	TRAVAIL
SEMBLANCE	CINQUEPACE	DAW	MELANCHOLY	INCITE
FLOUTING	COZENED	FREE SPACE	LECHERY	FRAY
SCRUPLE	SHREWD	REPROVE	OSTENTATION	RECKONING
DOUBLET	SIEVE	GALLANTS	CATECHIZING	CARPING

Much Ado Vocabulary

LIEGE	SEXTON	DISSEMBLER	INFAMY	DEFILED
KNAVE	THWARTING	ARRAS	OMINOUS	PERTURBATION
CUDGELED	PONIARDS	FREE SPACE	REDEMPTION	MALEFACTORS
AGATE	PLEACHED	BETROTHS	APPERTAIN	COXCOMB
VICTUAL	TARTLY	LEAGUE	FOILS	WANTON

Much Ado Vocabulary

HAGGARDS	OSTENTATION	CONSTABLE	COZENED	SCRUPLE
MANIFEST	INFAMY	SIEVE	CODPIECE	SLANDERED
HEARKEN	MARL	FREE SPACE	FRAY	COVERTLY
CAPON	PIETY	REDEMPTION	DOTE	CLAMOR
ARRAS	CUCKOLD	ENFRANCHISED	INTERMINGLE	BETROTHS

Much Ado Vocabulary

VARLET	EPITHET	REQUITED	DISPARAGE	MALEFACTORS
VICTUAL	COMMODITY	LIBERTINES	RENDER	ENIGMATICAL
COXCOMB	FOLLIES	FREE SPACE	CUDGELED	VOUCHSAFE
PESTILENCE	EXPEDIENT	PLEACHED	ORTHOGRAPHY	FOILS
QUALM	TURNCOAT	LECHERY	TARTLY	BETWIXT

Much Ado Vocabulary

THWARTING	VOUCHSAFE	VALOR	LEAGUE	TARTLY
CAPON	DISPARAGE	APPERTAIN	REPROVE	PERADVENTURE
MORTIFYING	ORTHOGRAPHY	FREE SPACE	SIEVE	OBSTINATE
LIEGE	SCRUPLE	MALEFACTORS	RENDER	COZENED
FOLLIES	INTERMINGLE	PERFUMER	ARRAS	VARLET

Much Ado Vocabulary

SHREWD	DISSEMBLER	DAW	DISSUADE	REQUITED
COVERTLY	ANGLING	SLANDERED	AGATE	ENSUING
MELANCHOLY	EPITHET	FREE SPACE	PONIARDS	CODPIECE
CONSTABLE	SEDGES	CINQUEPACE	FLOUTING	GALLANTS
SEMBLANCE	DEFILED	QUALM	EXPEDIENT	PLEACHED

Much Ado Vocabulary

ENFRANCHISED	PERJURY	LIEGE	VALOR	TARTLY
VICTUAL	SCRUPLE	CONSTABLE	MALEFACTORS	PRECEPTIAL
APPERTAIN	RECKONING	FREE SPACE	RENDER	COVERTLY
ACCORDANT	HAVOC	CUDGELED	HEARKEN	DAW
CUCKOLD	CAPON	REQUITED	TABOR	PESTILENCE

Much Ado Vocabulary

TEDIOUS	PLEACHED	ENSUING	OMINOUS	LEAGUE
FLOUTING	MELANCHOLY	HAGGARDS	SEDGES	AGATE
VARLET	TURNCOAT	FREE SPACE	SLANDERED	INCITE
PERADVENTURE	KNAVE	THWARTING	ANGLING	LECHERY
SEMBLANCE	DISPARAGE	COMMODITY	PERNICIOUS	FOILS

Much Ado Vocabulary

FOLLIES	MALEFACTORS	COZENED	CLAMOR	VARLET
DOUBLET	VOUCHSAFE	MANIFEST	OSTENTATION	SQUARER
PIETY	ACCORDANT	FREE SPACE	PRECEPTIAL	SEMBLANCE
VICTUAL	INTERMINGLE	OBSTINATE	DISDAINED	PONIARDS
DISSEMBLER	DISSUADE	MARL	HAVOC	COMMODITY

Much Ado Vocabulary

SEXTON	TARTLY	LEAGUE	DISPARAGE	BETWIXT
HEARKEN	IMPEDIMENT	DAW	AGATE	CUCKOLD
INCITE	TRAVAIL	FREE SPACE	EPITHET	PERJURY
ENIGMATICAL	PERADVENTURE	ENSUING	CAPON	GALLANTS
CANKER	SLANDERED	CUDGELED	SEDGES	FOILS

Much Ado Vocabulary

GALLANTS	REDEMPTION	VICTUAL	FOLLIES	MALEFACTORS
INFAMY	APPERTAIN	PERJURY	THWARTING	INCITE
CLAMOR	AGATE	FREE SPACE	SHREWD	CUDGELED
CATECHIZING	OMINOUS	REPROVE	DISSUADE	OSTENTATION
PRECEPTIAL	EXPEDIENT	EPITHET	FLOUTING	COMMODITY

Much Ado Vocabulary

VOUCHSAFE	PESTILENCE	SQUARER	LEAGUE	TARTLY
OBSTINATE	LIBERTINES	BETROTHS	PERFUMER	CONSTABLE
TURNCOAT	DISDAINED	FREE SPACE	PERNICIOUS	CANKER
HAVOC	PONIARDS	REQUITED	DOUBLET	MORTIFYING
SCRUPLE	MANIFEST	BETWIXT	HITHER	ENIGMATICAL

Much Ado Vocabulary

TABOR	COZENED	VALOR	AGATE	EPITHET
CONSTABLE	DISSUADE	DAW	OMINOUS	LIEGE
HAGGARDS	PERJURY	FREE SPACE	VOUCHSAFE	LEAGUE
LIBERTINES	GALLANTS	SLANDERED	VICTUAL	ACCORDANT
OSTENTATION	KNAVE	VARLET	TEDIOUS	MARL

Much Ado Vocabulary

RENDER	REDEMPTION	DISSEMBLER	EXPEDIENT	RECKONING
HEARKEN	ORTHOGRAPHY	TRAVAIL	CODPIECE	SHREWD
CUCKOLD	DOTE	FREE SPACE	ANGLING	DISDAINED
FRAY	PRECEPTIAL	PERTURBATION	QUALM	TARTLY
HITHER	PERADVENTURE	CAPON	COVERTLY	DISPARAGE

www.ingramcontent.com/pod-product-compliance
Lightning Source LLC
LaVergne TN
LVHW081536060526
838200LV00048B/2101